This Book Belongs to

_____

10th Anniversary
Content and Artwork by
Gooseberry Patch Company

LEISURE ARTS

Vice President and Editor-in-Chief: Sandra Graham Case
Managing Editor: Susan White Sullivan
Designer Relations Director: Debra Nettles
Craft Publications Director: Deb Moore
Art Publications Director: Rhonda Shelby
Knit and Crochet Director: Cheryl Johnson
Design Director: Cyndi Hansen
Special Projects Director: Susan Frantz Wiles
Senior Prepress Director: Mark Hawkins

EDITORIAL STAFF

TECHNICAL
Senior Technical Writer: Christina Kirkendoll
Technical Associates: Joan Beebe, Katie Galucki, Joyce Scott Harris and Laura Siar Holyfield

EDITORIAL
Editorial Writer: Susan McManus Johnson

FOODS
Foods Editor: Jane Kenner Prather
Foods Assistant Editor: Laura Siar Holyfield
Contributing Test Kitchen Staff: Rose Glass Klein

DESIGN
Design Captain: Anne Pulliam Stocks
Designers: Kim Hamblin, Kelly Reider, Lori Wenger and Becky Werle

ART
Art Category Manager: Lora Puls
Lead Graphic Artist: Jeanne Zaffarano
Graphic Artists: Frances Huddleston, Angela Ormsby Stark, Amy Temple, Dana Vaughn and Janie Wright
Imaging Technicians: Brian Hall, Stephanie Johnson and Mark R. Potter
Photography Manager: Katherine Atchison
Staff Photographer: Lloyd Litsey
Contributing Photo Stylist: Christy Myers
Publishing Systems Administrator: Becky Riddle
Publishing Systems Assistants: Clint Hanson and John Rose

BUSINESS STAFF

Vice President and Chief Operations Officer: Tom Siebenmorgen
Corporate Planning and Development Director: Laticia Mull Dittrich
Vice President, Sales and Marketing: Pam Stebbins
National Accounts Director: Martha Adams
Sales and Services Director: Margaret Reinold
Information Technology Director: Hermine Linz
Controller: Laura Ogle
Vice President, Operations: Jim Dittrich
Comptroller, Operations: Rob Thieme
Retail Customer Service Manager: Stan Raynor
Print Production Manager: Fred F. Pruss

OXMOOR HOUSE

Editor-in-Chief: Nancy Fitzpatrick Wyatt
Executive Editor: Susan Carlisle Payne
Foods Editor: Kelly Hooper Troiano
Photography Director: Jim Bathie
Associate Photo Stylist: Katherine Eckert
Test Kitchens Director: Elizabeth Tyler Austin
Test Kitchens Assistant Director: Julie Christopher
Test Kitchens Professionals: Kathleen Royal Phillips, Catherine Crowell Steele and Ashley T. Strickland
Test Kitchens Interns: Carol Corbin and Patty Michaud
Contributing Test Kitchens Professionals: Jane Chambliss and Kate Wheeler, R.D.
Contributing Food Stylists: Ana Kelly and Debby Maugans
Contributing Photographers: Beau Gustafson and Lee Harrelson

Library of Congress Catalog Number 99-71586
Hardcover ISBN 0-84873-226-X   Softcover ISBN 0-84873-237-5

10 9 8 7 6 5 4 3 2 1

Christmas
10th Anniversary

Christmas

Gooseberry Patch

To our dear friends & family...thanks for
10 years of food, friendship & fun!

MERRY CHRISTMAS

How Did Gooseberry Patch Get Started?

Y ou may know the story of Gooseberry Patch...the tale of two country friends who decided one day over the backyard fence to try their hands at the mail order business. Started in JoAnn's kitchen back in 1984, Vickie & JoAnn's dream of a "Country Store in Your Mailbox" has grown and grown to a 96-page catalog with over 400 products, including cookie cutters, Santas, snowmen, gift baskets, angels and our very own line of cookbooks! What an adventure for two country friends!

T hrough our catalogs and books, Gooseberry Patch has met country friends from all over the world. While sharing letters and phone calls, we found that our friends love to cook, decorate, garden and craft. We've created Kate, Holly & Mary Elizabeth to represent these devoted friends who live and love the country lifestyle the way we do. They're just like you & me... they're our "Country Friends®!"

Your friends at Gooseberry Patch

Mary Elizabeth ★ Holly ★ Kate ★ Spot

Table of contents

Here We Come A-Caroling

You can't help but hum your favorite Christmas tunes as you make these joyful ideas, so just imagine how much fun you'll have at your neighborhood caroling party! Hang the invitations on doorknobs up and down the street…it's time to whip up festive music books, candles and more for a cozy Christmas choir. With the promise of cocoa and cookies at the end of the evening, the whole gang will enjoy the merriment of a holiday sing-along.

Caroling Invitation instructions are on page 120.

Join us for Caroling!

Meet at the Kern home

25 Oakwood Lane

Saturday, December 22nd

At 7:00 in the evening.

Caroling Invitation

Songbook

Candle Cuff

The happy sounds of Christmas are reason enough to celebrate. Add bell-trimmed Songbooks, colorful Candle Cuffs and knitted Winter Warmers (shown on page 15), and everyone will warm up to the idea of singing their best.

Songbooks

For each book, print Christmas songs on 8¹/₂"x11" cardstock. Make an 8¹/₂"x11" scrapbook paper cover and decorate with glitter and alphabet rubber stamps. Punch holes through the pages and the cover. Adding a jingle bell at each hole, tie the book together with twill tape and wired pom-pom trim.

Candle Cuffs

Use the pattern on page 146 and make layered cardstock and scrapbook paper cuffs. Add glitter and wired pom-pom trim as you'd like. For the opening, use a craft knife to cut along the center lines where shown on the pattern. Slide each cuff over the top of a taper candle.

11

Glowing Walkway Lanterns light the way as the Christmas carolers arrive at your home. A Wintry Arrangement displayed on a washboard and a cheery Noel Sign are farmhouse-style decorations sure to make everyone feel welcome.

Wintry Arrangement

12   Walkway Lanterns

Walkway Lanterns

- tin snips
- protective gloves
- copper flashing
- hammer and awl
- 1/4" dia. gold brads
- 18-gauge coated wire
- needle-nose pliers
- wide-mouth quart-size canning jars with candles

Don't leave burning candles unattended.

1. For each lantern, enlarge the patterns on page 146 to 165%. Use the patterns and cut a lantern top and bottom from flashing.
2. Use the awl to punch holes in the top and bottom where shown on the patterns and then randomly on the top as desired. Bend the top into a cone and secure with brads.
3. Cut three 30" wire lengths. Twist the wires together at one end to make a 2½"-long hanging loop. Curl the wire ends below the loop. Thread the lantern top and bottom onto the wires with the jar in between. Curl the wire ends at the bottom of the lantern to secure.

Wintry Arrangement
Instructions are on page 120.

Noel Sign

- 49"x11"x³/₄" board
- hammer
- plain and upholstery nails
- 2" hinge with screws
- burnt umber and other assorted acrylic paint colors
- paintbrushes
- sandpaper
- 9¹/₂"-tall wooden letters (NOEL)
- tin snips
- protective gloves and goggles
- galvanized metal and copper sheets
- wire mesh screen
- wood glue
- staple gun
- drill with bits
- screwdriver
- 3³/₈"x42" fence picket or board
- matte clear acrylic spray sealer

1. Distress the board as desired by denting and scratching with the hammer, nails and screws. Brush thinned burnt umber paint over the board; wipe off the excess with paper towels, and then dry brush with burnt umber. Sand the board and repeat painting and sanding until you like how it looks.

2. Measure and mark four 10"wx11"h areas along the center of the board. Using both dark and light shades of the color, paint each area a different color. Dry brush the areas with burnt umber and add more distressing as desired.

3. Using the wooden letters as patterns, cut a piece from the metal sheets or screen to fit on the front of each letter. Paint the wooden letters and glue them to the board. Nail or staple the metal letters in place.

4. Drill pilot holes; then, use the hinge to attach the straight end of the picket to the center back of the sign, 10" from the top.

5. Apply sealer to the sign in a well-ventilated area.

Noel Sign

Jingle Bell Sugar Cookies

Royal Icing transforms these sugar cookies into jingle bells.

1 c. butter, softened
1 c. sugar
1 c. sour cream
2 eggs, beaten
2 t. vanilla extract
5 c. all-purpose flour
1 T. nutmeg
2 t. baking powder
1 1/4 t. salt
1 t. baking soda
Royal Icing

Beat butter and sugar until fluffy; set aside. Stir together sour cream, eggs and vanilla; mix well and set aside.

Combine flour, nutmeg, baking powder, salt and baking soda. Add flour mixture alternately with egg mixture to the butter mixture; blend well. Chill 2 hours.

Roll out dough, a softball-size amount at a time, on a floured surface with a floured rolling pin. Roll out to 1/8-inch thickness; cut using a 2 3/4-inch round cookie cutter. Arrange cookies on ungreased baking sheets. Bake at 375 degrees for 9 to 10 minutes or until just golden on bottoms. Cool completely on wire racks. Decorate with Royal Icing. Makes 7 dozen.

Ginnie Wible
McMurray, PA

Royal Icing:
5 1/3 c. powdered sugar
1/2 c. water
4 T. meringue powder
2 t. clear vanilla extract
black, yellow and red paste food coloring

Jingle Jingle Jingle

Beat powdered sugar, water, meringue powder and vanilla in a medium bowl at high speed with an electric mixer 7 to 10 minutes or until stiff. Divide icing evenly into 2 small bowls. Take 2 tablespoons from each bowl and place in another small bowl; tint black. Tint remaining icing yellow and red. Spoon each icing into a pastry bag fitted with a small round tip. Use red and yellow icing to outline and fill in cookies to resemble jingle bells. Pipe black icing for detail lines on jingle bells. Let icing harden.

Mug Cozy

Instructions begin on page 120.

Caroling Cocoa Mix

Hot chocolate always makes any occasion warmer!

1/2 c. sugar
2 T. whole almonds
1-oz. sq. bittersweet baking
    chocolate, chopped
1/4 c. baking cocoa
1/2 t. vanilla powder
1 t. cinnamon
1/2 t. ground cloves
1 c. milk for each serving
Garnish: whipped cream

Place sugar and almonds in a food processor; process until almonds are finely ground. Add next 5 ingredients; process until mixture is finely ground. Store in an airtight container. Makes 16 servings.

For each serving, add one tablespoon cocoa mix to one cup hot milk; whisk until frothy. Garnish with a dollop of whipped cream, if desired.

Winter Warmers

Instructions begin on page 121.

Jingle Bell Sugar Cookies
Caroling Cocoa Mix
Mug Cozy

Winter Warmers

sucH A merry Sight to See

Bells ringing on the door and reindeer dashing around the tree…an old-fashioned Christmas is so much fun to see! For merry memories you'll love to recall, set the holiday scene with easy handmade ornaments, a cheery reindeer tree skirt and a forest of little trees. This year's Yuletide cheer begins right here!

Wreath and Bell Ornament instructions are on page 125.

Felt Candy Ornament

- red, pink and white felt
- straight pins
- sturdy milliner's needle
- two ¼" dia. red beads
- red embroidery floss

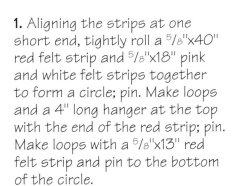

1. Aligning the strips at one short end, tightly roll a ⁵/₈"x40" red felt strip and ⁵/₈"x18" pink and white felt strips together to form a circle; pin. Make loops and a 4" long hanger at the top with the end of the red strip; pin. Make loops with a ⁵/₈"x13" red felt strip and pin to the bottom of the circle.

2. Thread a bead onto the center of a 22" floss length (use 3 strands). Thread both floss ends through the milliner's needle, and then run the floss through the ornament top loops, circle and bottom loops, adding a bead inside the last bottom loop. Thread the floss back through the bottom loops, the circle and the top loops. Knot and trim the floss below the top bead. Remove the pins.

Chenille Candy Canes
Instructions are on page 125.

Felt Candy Ornament

A truly quick & easy design to make is the Felt Candy Ornament with its swirl of red, pink and white. And here's a new twist on an old favorite…giant Chenille Candy Canes! The oversize craft stems can be found in many craft supply stores.

Chenille Candy Canes

Santa's reindeer dash around a needle-felted tree skirt that's sure to become a family heirloom. The fast technique is easy to do…a felting needle tool punches the yarn fibers into the felt for a permanent bond. So easy, so beautiful!

Tree Skirt

- 2 yds of 72"w cream felt
- 1³/₄ yds of 60"w red felt
- string
- thumbtack
- fabric marking pen
- transfer paper
- felting needle tool and mat
- cream and red wool yarn
- liquid fray preventative
- six 2" dia. self-covered buttons
- craft knife and cutting mat

Read *Needle Felting* on page 141 before beginning. Enlarge the patterns on pages 147-148 to 222%.

1. For the skirt, cut a 67" cream felt square. Follow *Making a Fabric Circle* on page 141 and use a 32¹/₂" string measurement to mark the outer cutting line. Remove the tack and use a 2" string measurement to mark the inner cutting line.

2. Repeat Step 1 with a 58" red felt square, using a 28", then 5" string measurement to mark the cutting lines.

3. Cut through all felt layers along the drawn lines. Unfold the circles. Use the wave pattern and cut a wavy outer edge on the red circle. Cut a side opening in each circle from the outer edge to the center opening.

(continued on page 126)

Tree Skirt

Tree Topper

Make a topper for your tree, and trees to top a table! A colorful felt Tree Topper is brightened with fabric yo-yos and buttons, while the whimsical woodland scene is also created from felt and fabric. The tall Cone Tree is made from a sweater sleeve...oh-so clever!

Tree Topper

- red stiffened felt
- white and red wool felt
- fabric glue or felting needle tool and mat
- print fabric scraps
- two 1 1/8" dia. red buttons
- three 1/2" dia. beads
- red embroidery floss
- white and green wool yarn
- polyester fiberfill

1. Enlarge the pattern on page 149 to 193%. Use the pattern and cut 2 large tree topper pieces from stiffened felt for the base. Cut the medium piece from white wool felt and the small piece from red wool felt.
2. Layer and glue or *Needle Felt* (page 141) the wool felt pieces to the center of one base.
3. Cut a 5 1/2" and a 7" diameter fabric circle. Make *Yo-Yos* (page 141) from the circles. Sewing a button and bead at the center of each, sew the Yo-Yos to the topper as shown. Glue or *Needle Felt* yarn to the topper as you'd like. Sew a bead to the top of the topper.
4. Leaving the bottom point open, sew the bases together along the outer edges. Stuff the top and middle sections only.

Yo-Yo, Felt Triangle and Cone Trees
Instructions are on pages 126-127.

Yo-Yo Trees
Felt Triangle Tree
Cone Trees

A Natural Noel

The best kind of Christmas is one that's unhurried and filled with simple country pleasures. This is just that kind of holiday…combine fragrant greenery, bright red berries and pinecones with some of your favorite things, and you have the beginning of a very merry Christmas. White dishes, a vintage watering can and a farmhouse table are some of our favorites…take a look, and you'll see just how easy it is!

Barn Wreath instructions are on page 127.

Barn Wreath

Hanging Basket Arrangement

Fill your home with the fresh scent of evergreen boughs this Christmas. Simply gather greenery to make your own arrangements…it's easy!

Fresh Greenery Bouquets

When cutting greenery, protect the health of the trees or shrubs by cutting boughs at an angle. This prevents moisture from standing on the exposed wood. Harvest the boughs discreetly, without taking too many from one side of a tree or shrub. Keep the cut ends of the boughs in water until you can arrange them.

Use any kind of container you have on hand to hold your arrangement. Water-absorbing florist's foam will make your greenery last longer. Soak the foam in water for a few hours before using it. Fill the bottom of your container with wet foam (line baskets with plastic first). For a shallow container, florist's tape or wire will help support the boughs. Criss-cross the tape or wire over the opening of the container and secure it around the container's rim. Insert the boughs into the foam.

If the back of your arrangement won't be seen, place the taller boughs in the back of the container. Otherwise, stand them in the middle and add shorter boughs all around. Enjoy the wintry fragrance of your evergreen creation!

Hanging Basket Arrangement

Place moistened, water-absorbing florist's foam inside a hanging basket (lined with plastic). Arrange fresh pine needles, arborvitae and holly in the foam and tuck in a few pinecones.

25

 An assortment of white dishes and silver pieces will make your mantel glow. Place pots of boxwood in a few of the larger pieces and add pinecones, candles (burn candles with caution), fresh greenery and garlands of shells and pinecones. You can make your own pinecone garland by tying and hot gluing different-sized pinecones to the ends of a twill tape length.

And remember, no matter where you go, there you are.

-CONFUCIUS-

Mirror Centerpiece

Place a potted boxwood shrub in a white crock and arrange on an antique framed mirror along with white glass dishes and silver pieces. Add pinecones, candles, fresh greenery and mirrored glass balls (don't leave burning candles unattended).

Mirror Centerpiece

Gift Giving

Giving packages a heartfelt touch is oh-so easy. Simply using pretty papers and ribbons, adding pinecone halves, a jingle bell or even tying on vintage finds like an old key make all the difference. Dress up layered tags with glittery pens, a mica star and easy-to-use rub-on greetings. Arranged in a wire basket with fresh greenery, packages look delightful while waiting to be given.

Welcome Sign

Simple embroidery and sewing will quickly create a Christmas quilt, a friendly welcome sign and a button-embellished wish for holiday cheer. The pillows are also done in a twinkle. Even easier are the trims for the little tree…lengths of rickrack and covered buttons are perfect partners for vintage-style ornaments. Add a few of your favorite things, and rest assured your guests will enjoy sweet Yuletide dreams!

Welcome Sign instructions are on page 127.

Embroidered Framed Piece

At Christmas.
play and
make good cheer,
for Christmas
comes but once
a year.

-Thomas Tusser

There's something sweet & simple about red and white together. This Embroidered Framed Piece features easy stitching. Buttons covered in printed fabrics pair up nicely with the swirls of Stem Stitches and French Knots. When you're ready to trim the guest room tree, create garlands of rickrack. Fabric-covered buttons look like ornaments while keeping the rickrack in place on the branches. Don't forget to arrange your Christmas collectibles or favorite toys under the tree.

Tabletop Tree

Embroidered Framed Piece
Instructions begin on page 127.

Tabletop Tree
Cover assorted sizes of self-covered buttons with fabric scraps. Spacing evenly and mixing sizes, thread the buttons onto green mini rickrack. For the garland, glue the buttons on the mini rickrack to red jumbo rickrack, letting the mini rickrack swag between the buttons. Randomly glue more covered buttons to the garland. Wrap the garland around the tree and fill in with green jumbo rickrack. Decorate the tree with vintage ornaments and an oversized covered-button tree topper.

Scrap Quilt

This red and white quilt will fill you with cheer! Stitching the sweet design is truly easy. Maybe you'd like to fashion coordinating pillows with simple appliqués and a little gathered fabric?

Corduroy Pillow

- $^2/_3$ yd red corduroy
- 18" square pillow form
- red and white print fabric scraps
- 2" dia. self-covered button
- upholstery needle
- $1^1/_8$" dia. button

1. Matching right sides and leaving a large opening in the bottom for stuffing, sew two 19" corduroy squares together with a $^1/_2$" seam allowance. For Turkish corners, leave a 3" tail and sew *Running Stitches* (page 142) across each corner $^1/_2$" in from the stitching. Gather and knot the beginning tail and thread ends together. Turn right side out, insert the pillow form and sew the opening closed.
2. Cut a 6" and an 8" diameter circle from the fabric scraps. Make Yo-Yos (page 141) from the circles.
3. Cover the 2" button with corduroy. Beginning at the center back of the pillow, insert the needle through the $1^1/_8$" button, the pillow, the Yo-Yos and the covered button at the front. Take the needle back through the Yo-Yos, pillow and back button. Pull the thread tight and tie at the back to tuft.

Scrap Quilt and Holly Pillow
Instructions are on pages 128-129.

Corduroy Pillow
Holly Pillow

What would make your guests feel more at home than finding stockings full of goodies awaiting their arrival? Fill sweetly stitched stockings with gift cards, toys or other treats they may need during their stay. So thoughtful!

Corduroy Stocking

- ³/₄ yd red corduroy
- ³/₄ yd red print fabric for lining
- white rickrack
- white embroidery floss
- 10" length of 1½"w red twill tape
- 1⅛" dia. self-covered button

Match right sides and use a ½" seam allowance.

1. Enlarge the pattern on page 150 to 222%. Excluding the zigzags, use the pattern and cut 2 corduroy stocking pieces (one in reverse) and 2 print fabric lining pieces (one in reverse).
2. Sew rickrack; then, add *Running Stitches* (page 142) with 6 strands of floss across one stocking piece near the top as shown.
3. Leaving the top open, sew the stocking pieces together; clip the curves and turn right side out. Repeat for the lining, leaving an opening in the side for turning; do not turn the lining right side out. Matching raw edges, place the stocking in the lining.
4. For the hanger, match long edges and fold the twill tape in half. Sew the long edges together; then, add *Running Stitches* with 6 strands of floss.
5. Matching raw edges, place the hanger between the stocking and lining at the heel-side seam. Sew the pieces together along the top edges. Turn right side out through the opening in the lining and sew the opening closed. Tuck the lining in the stocking.
6. Make a Yo-Yo (page 141) from a 5½" diameter print fabric circle.
7. Cover the button with corduroy. Stack and sew the Yo-Yo and button to the stocking front.

Zigzag Stocking

- ³/₈ yd white fabric
- ³/₄ yd red corduroy
- ³/₄ yd red print fabric for lining
- clear nylon thread
- white embroidery floss
- 10" length of 1½"w red twill tape
- 1⅛" dia. self-covered button
- red and white print fabric scrap

Match right sides and use a ½" seam allowance.

1. Enlarge the pattern on page 150 to 222%. Use the pattern and cut the stocking front from white fabric and the stocking back (in reverse) from corduroy. Cut 2 lining pieces (one in reverse) from the lining fabric.
2. Cut the zigzag pieces from corduroy and zigzag them to the stocking front with clear thread. Sew *Running Stitches* (page 142) along the zigzag edges with 6 strands of floss.
3. Follow steps 3-5 of the Corduroy Stocking to assemble the stocking.
4. Make a Yo-Yo (page 141) from a 5½" diameter lining fabric circle.
5. Cover the button with the fabric scrap. Stack and sew the Yo-Yo and button to the stocking front.

Corduroy Stocking
Zigzag Stocking

Christmas Keepsakes

Memorabilia Tablescape

The toy reindeer Grandma gave you, the jolly Santa figure that watches over your celebrations...the holidays just wouldn't be right without your family's sweet keepsakes. Add to the season's memories by creating simple stockings, an old-time pull toy or a soft Santa doll. And for a fun way to display your vintage holiday decorations, turn a picture frame into a festive tray for a tablescape.

Memorabilia Tablescape instructions are on page 129.

Santa Doll

Remember the excitement of visiting Santa Claus and telling him all your Christmas wishes? How about a fun-to-make replica of the jolly gentleman?

Santa Doll

- $7/8$ yd red velveteen fabric
- $1/4$ yd muslin
- polyester fiberfill
- tracing paper
- fabric glue
- $1/8$ yd faux sheep wool
- $1/2$"x$7/8$" gold buckle
- $1/2$ yd of $3/8$"w black ribbon
- $1/16$" dia. hole punch
- two $1/4$" dia. black shank buttons
- blush and applicator
- $1/4$ yd white faux fur
- $1^3/4$" dia. white pom-pom

Match right sides and use a $1/4$" seam allowance.

1. Enlarge the patterns on pages 151-152 to 222%. Use the patterns and cut a body and a full body/head piece from velveteen and a head from muslin.

2. Sew the body and head pieces together; then, sew them to the full body/head piece, leaving the bottom edge open. Clip the curves. Turn right side out and stuff. Sew across the arms where they meet the body to form the shoulder joints.

3. Use the leg pattern and cut 4 legs (2 in reverse) from velveteen. Leaving the top edges open, sew the legs together in pairs. Clip the curves. Turn right side out and stuff, stopping 2" from the openings. Sew across the legs 2" from the openings. Arrange and pin the legs at the bottom of the body. Catching the legs in the stitching, sew the body opening closed.

4. For the collar, matching the top corners at the front, wrap and glue a $2^1/4$"x$12^1/2$" wool strip around Santa's neck and shoulders. Glue $1^1/4$" wide wool strips around the wrists and ankles.

5. For the belt, thread the buckle onto one end of the ribbon and glue $1/2$" of the end to the back. Punch a hole $1^3/4$" from the opposite ribbon end for buckling the belt. Securing in spots with glue, wrap and buckle the belt around Santa's body.

6. Sew the buttons to the face for the eyes. Blush the cheeks. Cut the eyebrows, beard and 2 mustache pieces from faux fur and glue them to the face.

7. Use the hat pattern and cut 2 velveteen hat pieces. Sew the sides together, clip the point and turn right side out. Glue a $1^1/4$" wide wool strip along the bottom of the hat and the pom-pom to the top point. Glue the hat to Santa's head.

Joy Pull Toy

Make a holiday pull toy to celebrate all those Christmas mornings when you couldn't wait to look under the tree. These fun felt stockings are also nostalgic, reminding us of the stocking kits we put together as children.

Joy Pull Toy
- wood glue
- 5" tall wooden letters (2 of each)
- wood filler
- sandpaper
- acrylic paints
- paintbrushes
- three $3^3/4$"x$3^3/4$"x$^{11}/16$" wooden blocks
- twelve $1^1/2$" dia. wooden wheels
- decoupage glue
- scrapbook papers

- drill with bits
- screwdriver
- three $1^1/4$" long screws and twelve 1" long screws
- $^1/4$" dia. hole punch
- cardstock
- five $^3/4$" long screw eyes
- 7" length of string
- $^5/8$" dia. wooden bead
- two $^5/8$" "S" hooks

1. Stack and glue the letters together in pairs. Allow to dry; then, smooth the seams with wood filler. Sand the letters.
2. Paint the letters, blocks and wheels.
3. Using decoupage glue, cover the top of each block and the front and back of each letter with scrapbook papers; lightly sand the paper edges. Brush glue over the blocks and letters.

4. Drill a pilot hole through the center of each block and $^1/2$" into the bottom of each letter; then, attach a letter to each block with a $1^1/4$" screw.
5. Mark the wheel placement $^3/4$" from the corners on two sides of each block. Drill pilot holes; then, attach the wheels with 1" screws. Don't tighten the screws so much that the wheels won't turn. Glue punched cardstock circles to the ends of the wheel screws.
6. Drilling pilot holes if needed, center and attach the screw eyes on the remaining sides of the blocks (front only on the "Y" block). Knot one string end, thread the bead onto the string and knot the other end to the screw eye at the front of the "J" block. Join the blocks with the "S" hooks.

Felt Stockings
Instructions are on page 130.

Felt Stockings

Handmade Happiness to Share

One-of-a-kind gifts always warm hearts, so why not skip long hours of shopping in favor of creating handmade presents? From linens to aprons and button jewelry to thoughtful things for the gardener...great ideas for clever gifts can be found on these pages. A reversible doll, bright-colored pincushions and painted reindeer tumblers all provide extra cheer.

Evergreen Spray instructions are on page 130.

Evergreen Spray

Keeping tidy never looked so good! A farmhouse style apron with a handy pocket is a thoughtful gift. And you surely know a little someone who would love to help with the baking, if only she had a vinyl-covered apron like this one to keep her tidy.

Child's Apron

Child's Apron
- tracing paper
- ¹/₂ yd fabric for apron
- ¹/₂ yd clear vinyl
- 2 yds of ³/₄"w rickrack
- clear nylon thread
- ¹/₄ yd red and white polka-dot fabric
- scrap of green fabric
- fabric glue
- 2¹/₂ yds of 1¹/₂"w twill tape
- liquid fray preventative

Our apron is 13¹/₄"x20". You may need to adjust the size of your apron to fit your child.

1. Enlarge the pocket and apron half patterns on page 153 to 196%. Read *Making Patterns* on page 141, and extending the bottom edge 9", make a whole apron pattern. Use the pattern and cut an apron from fabric and vinyl.
2. Place the vinyl apron on top of the fabric apron. Pin rickrack along the edges. Sew the apron together with nylon thread.
3. For the pocket, use the pattern and cut a whole strawberry from polka-dot fabric and vinyl and the cap from green fabric. Glue the cap to the strawberry. Sew the vinyl to the front of the strawberry. Leaving the top open, zigzag the pocket to the apron with nylon thread.
4. Cut a 21" twill tape length for the neck strap. Press the ends ¹/₂" to the back twice. Sewing through the rickrack, sew the pressed ends to the top corners at the back of the apron.
5. For the ties, cut two 33" twill tape lengths. Press one end of each tie ¹/₂" to the back twice. Apply fray preventative to the opposite end. Sewing through the rickrack, sew the pressed end of a tie to each side of the apron back at the top of the straight side edge.

Grownup Apron
Instructions are on page 130.

Reindeer Tumblers

- clear self-adhesive laminate
- clear glass tumblers
- craft knife and cutting mat
- brown spray paint
- black, red and white glass paints
- small paintbrushes
- cotton swabs

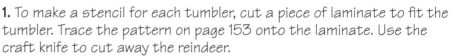

These tumblers should be handwashed only. Leave at least 1" unpainted at the top of each tumbler.

Perfect gifts for your host or hostess, these beverage servers will keep them refreshed all season long. The designs on the glass Reindeer Tumblers are simple to create using stencils. And anyone can keep tea, coffee or cocoa warm with a Christmas Cozy fashioned from a cast-off sweater.

1. To make a stencil for each tumbler, cut a piece of laminate to fit the tumbler. Trace the pattern on page 153 onto the laminate. Use the craft knife to cut away the reindeer.
2. Adhere the stencil to the tumbler, smoothing out any wrinkles. Working in a well-ventilated area, spray a light coat of brown paint over the stencil. Allow to dry; then, carefully remove the stencil.
3. Paint the eyes, nose and collar and use a cotton swab to add white dots for snow. Allow the tumblers to dry for several days before using.

Reindeer Tumblers

48

Christmas Cozy

- tightly-woven sweater
- teapot or coffee pot
- fabric scraps
- snowflake buttons
- large-eye needle
- ¹/₈"w ribbon

Match right sides and use a ¹/₄" seam allowance.

1. Using the finished edge as the bottom edge, cut a piece from the bottom of the sweater 3" taller than the pot and large enough to wrap around the pot (excluding the handle and spout) plus 4".

2. Matching the side edges, fold the sweater piece in half; then, cut along the fold. With the finished edges at the bottom and leaving openings for the handle and spout, sew the sweater pieces together along the side edges. Turn right side out and hand sew the raw edges of the openings ¹/₄" to the wrong side.

3. Make Yo-Yos (page 141) with circles cut from fabric scraps (we used 4" diameter circles). Sewing a button at the center of each, sew the Yo-Yos to the front of the cozy.

4. Fold the bottom edge of the cozy 1¹/₂" to the right side. Sew Running Stitches (page 142) with ribbons around the cozy at the top of the folded area and ¹/₂" from the top edge. Place the cozy on the pot. Pull the ribbons tight to gather the fabric, tie each into a bow and trim the ends.

Christmas Cozy

Crochet-Trimmed Towels

- 21"x28" (53.5 cm x 71 cm) tea towels
- assorted buttons and/or pony beads
- cream cotton crochet thread, size 5
- size G (4 mm) crochet hook
- clear nylon thread

Read Crochet on pages 144-145 before beginning.

For each towel, thread 80 buttons/beads onto the crochet thread. Chain 85. Turn and crochet a whole row in *Single Crochet*. *Chain* 3 at the end and turn. *Double Crochet* in each *Single Crochet* to the end. *Chain* 3, slip a button or bead up the thread and *Double Crochet* in the next stitch. Slip a bead or button up and *Double Crochet* in the next stitch. Continue to the end, sliding a bead or button between the stitches; finish off. Wrapping any excess trim to the back, pin the trim along one short edge of the towel; then, zigzag in place with clear thread.

Gifts that add comfort to a home…who wouldn't enjoy owning a pair of kitchen towels edged with buttons or beads? The basic Crochet instructions on pages 144-145 make the towel trim easy enough for a beginner!

Crochet-Trimmed Towels

Here's an easy gift to make that's truly one-size-fits-all! The portable fleece blanket is washable and lightweight…features that hikers, stargazers, sports fans or anyone who enjoys spur-of-the-moment picnics can truly appreciate.

Fleece Throw to Go

- 50"x60" fleece throw
- ³/₈ yd print fabric
- pinking shears
- 14¹/₂" length of 1¹/₄"w cotton strapping

1. Fold the throw into thirds by folding in the long edges. Starting at one short end, roll up the throw.

2. For the ties, cut two 5"x32" fabric strips. Matching right sides and long edges, fold each strip in half. Sew the long raw edges together with a ¹/₂" seam allowance. Turn right side out and pink the short edges.

3. For the handle, fold 1" of each strapping end to the wrong side. Sandwich a tie, 8¹/₂" from one short end of the tie, in each folded handle end. Pin the handle ends to the top layer of the rolled throw, 3¹/₂" from the short end. Unfold the throw; then, sew the handle ends to the top layer. Refold the throw, wrap the ties around the throw and knot the ends to secure.

Fleece Throw to Go

Ripple Crocheted Throw

A crocheted throw will warm a loved one in body and soul. And a quick gift to fashion is the blossom-embellished denim jacket…no weekend wardrobe is complete without it!

Appliquéd Jacket
- fabric glue or clear nylon thread
- ¹/₈"w ribbon
- denim jacket
- tracing paper
- assorted colors of wool felt
- felting needle tool and mat (optional)
- coordinating embroidery floss

Glue or sew ribbon to the jacket as desired. Use the pattern on page 154 and cut the appliqué pieces from felt. Glue or *Needle Felt* (page 141) the pieces to the jacket; then, use 3 strands of floss to *Blanket Stitch* (page 142) along the edges of the pieces and add *Straight Stitches* and *French Knots*. Add sets of long *Straight Stitches* to the jacket as you'd like.

Ripple Crocheted Throw
Instructions begin on page 130.

Appliquéd Jacket

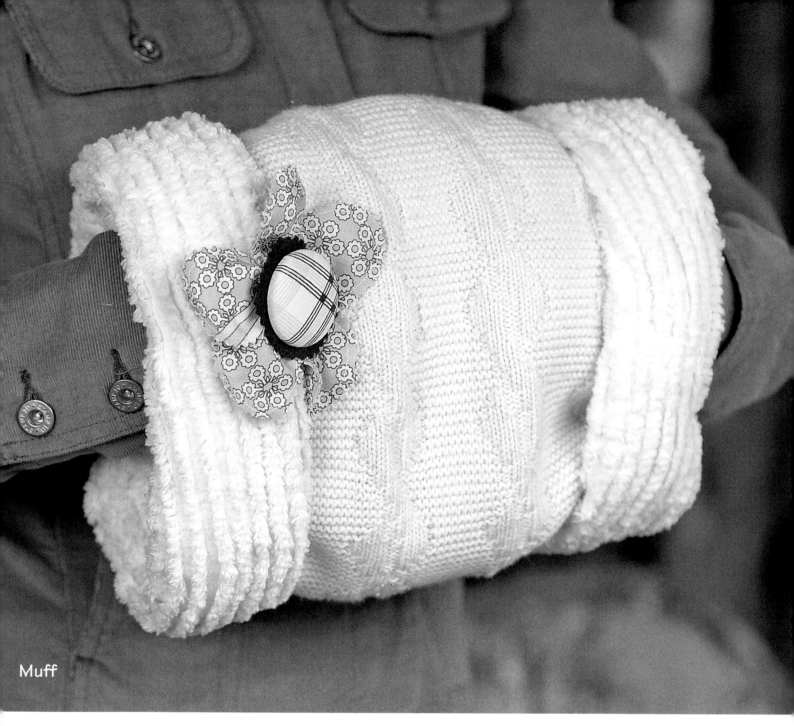

Muff

Don't toss out that favorite old sweater! It can still have a warm and useful life as a chenille-lined Muff. Make it pretty with a button-centered flower.

Muff
Instructions begin on page 131.

frosty fingers, rosy cheeks

54

More than just jewelry, the necklace and earrings are made using vintage buttons and beads. Why not fashion a set from your mom's or aunt's buttons and jewelry? It's a wonderful way to create sentimental gifts.

Button Jewelry

Necklace
- assorted beads and buttons
- three 2" headpins
- round-nose pliers
- 46" length of $1/8$" dia. rattail cord
- wire cutters
- hot glue gun

1. For the dangles, thread beads and buttons onto $3/4$" of the pins and use the pliers to tightly wrap the pin ends around the cord at the center. Trim the pin ends.
2. Thread both cord ends through a bead and slide the bead down to the dangles. Layering and gluing or sewing buttons together as desired, sew buttons to the cord (our large cream-colored button is a shank button with the shank removed).
3. For an adjustable closure, thread one cord end through 2 beads; knot the end. Thread the remaining cord end through the beads from the opposite side; knot the end. Trim the cord ends. Pull the beads away from each other to tighten the necklace.

Earrings
Thread beads and buttons onto $1^1/4$" of 2" headpins. Use round-nose pliers to tightly loop the pin ends onto earwires (our earwires are leverback).

Remember reversible dolls? Each one seemed ready-made for storytelling fun. This little doll may bring to mind the tale of Sleeping Beauty. Create the playtime friend for a special girl, and see where her imagination takes her.

Flip-Flop Doll
Instructions begin on page 132.

Pincushions

- assorted colors of felt
- coordinating embroidery floss
- sand
- fabric glue
- tracing paper
- 1" dia. shank buttons with shanks removed

Refer to Embroidery Stitches on page 142 before beginning. Use 3 strands of floss.

1. For each of the small pincushions, cut two 3" diameter felt circles and a 2"x9½" or a 2½"x9½" felt rectangle. For the large pincushion, cut two 3½" diameter felt circles and a 2½"x11" felt rectangle.

2. For each pincushion, sew the circles to the long edges of the rectangle with a ¼" seam allowance, leaving the short edges open. Turn right side out and Stem Stitch along the seams. Fill with sand and glue the opening closed.

3. Use the patterns on page 155 and cut felt flowers and leaves. Embroidering or adding buttons as desired, layer and glue or sew the flowers and leaves to the cushions.

Pincushions

You know your sewing friends will have fun using these colorful felt creations, but you'll have even more fun making the handy pincushions! Each totally unique gift is topped by one or more flower shapes. Choose your favorite buttons to add sparkle to the large blooms.

Help your gardening friend grow sweet memories along with her flowers! A pocketed apron made from vintage tea towels will help her keep track of garden necessities. Tucked into a wooden tray, a flowerpot and some bulbs are reminders that her favorite season is on its way.

Gardening apron

No matter how long the winter, spring is sure to follow

Merry Christmas !

Gardener's Gift Set

to Anne from Becky

Gardener's Gift Set
Instructions are on page 133.

Felted Granny Square Tote
Read Crochet on pages 144-145
before beginning.

Finished Size:
10½"w x 14"h x 3½"d
(26.5 cm x 35.5 cm x 9 cm)

⬤◧▢▢ **EASY**

Materials
Medium Weight
100% Wool Yarn
　　[3½ ounces, 210 yards
　　(100 grams, 192 meters)
　　per skein]:
　　　　Blue - 1 skein
　　　　Cream - 1 skein
　　　　Rose - 1 skein
　　　　Green - 3 skeins
Crochet hooks, size H (5 mm) **and**
　　K (6.5 mm) **or** size needed
　　for gauge
1⅛" (29 mm) Buttons - 4
Yarn needle
Lining fabric - ½ yard (45.5 cm)
Sewing needle and thread

Gauge: With smaller size hook,
　　each Square = 4¼" (10.75 cm)
　　before felting.

(continued on page 133)

Tags, Cards & Wrap

Treat yourself by sharing these tags, cards and wrapped presents with everyone you know. With the wide selection of papers available today, you can be sure you're creating original tags and cards. You'll also find fun ways to turn vintage fabrics into clever gift wraps! Many of these ideas are as easy as cutting, folding and embellishing, and each will become a treasured decoration for Christmases yet to come.

Tag Wreath instructions are on page 135.

Tag Wreath

There are so many thoughtful ways to say "Merry Christmas" with pretty papers! To share seasonal cheer, the Country Friends like to personalize gifts with package tie-ons whenever they can. Another favorite way to express heartfelt good wishes is with handmade greeting cards and gift card holders.

Ice Skate Package Tie-Ons

Doll-size ice skates make adorable package tie-ons. Write names or messages on little chipboard tags, slide the tags onto the skate laces and tie the skates onto your packages.

Merry Christmas Card

Instructions are on page 135.

Ice Skate Package Tie-Ons
Merry Christmas Card

Do Not Open Gift Card Holder
Ho Ho Ho Gift Card Holder

Do Not Open
Gift Card Holder

- craft glue
- scrapbook papers
- gift card
- rub-on message and snowflakes
- fine-point permanent pen
- photo corners
- $^3/_8$"w twill tape
- embroidery floss
- "Do not open" chipboard tag
- $^7/_8$" dia. button
- large plastic-coated paperclip

This side-fold card holder is two gifts in one! There's a gift card inside and the flower clip can be worn on a shirt or jacket or used as a bookmark.

1. For the card holder, glue two 3"x9" scrapbook paper pieces together back-to-back; then, fold in half, matching the short edges.

2. Gluing at the back, wrap a scrapbook paper strip around the gift card widthwise. Slide the card out of the strip.
3. Add rub-ons and dot the strip with the pen. Replace the gift card in the strip. Adhere the gift card inside the card holder with photo corners.
4. Gluing at the center, make a flower from 3" long twill tape loops. Thread floss through the hole in the tag, then the button holes and glue at the back. Glue the button to the flower front and the paperclip to the back. Clip the flower on the card holder to keep it closed.

Ho Ho Ho Gift Card Holder

- craft glue
- scrapbook papers
- gift card
- $^3/_8$"w twill tape
- rub-on message
- coordinating thread
- "Ho Ho Ho" embellishment

This pocket-style holder is quick and simple to make. The bow makes it easy to slide the gift card out.

1. Gluing at the back, wrap a scrapbook paper strip around the gift card lengthwise. Slide the card out of the strip.
2. For the bow, make a 1$^3/_4$" long twill tape loop. Wrapping and gluing one end around the center of the bow, glue a twill tape length around the scrapbook paper strip. Add the rub-on to the strip and replace the gift card.
3. For the pocket, cut two 2$^3/_4$"x4" scrapbook paper pieces. Zigzag along one short edge of each piece; then, zigzag the pieces together along the long and remaining short edges. Adhere the embellishment to the pocket front and insert the gift card.

When you can't spend Christmas with a loved one, send a photo card in your place! You'll still be missed, but they'll love seeing your smile. Even your gifts can display friendly faces when you put family photos on tags and bags.

Happiness Tag and Pocket

Dress up a blank library pocket and tag with vintage-look scrapbook paper, glitter, rickrack and stickers. Use photo corners to add a photo from Christmas past to the tag along with a rub-on message and tie on some jute twine. Line the envelope with scrapbook paper for an extra-special touch.

Photo Window Card

Instructions are on page 136.

Happiness Tag and Pocket
Photo Window Card

Photo Tag

Photo Tag

For the tag, cut a 3"x4³/4" cardstock piece, round one end and punch a ¹/4" diameter hole in the top (or use a tag die and a die-cutting tool). Layer and glue 3" and 2¹/2" diameter wavy-edged scrapbook paper circles and a 2" diameter photo on the tag. Add a name with cardstock stickers and use adhesive foam dots to attach a chipboard message. Knot ribbon through the hole in the tag.

Holiday Memories Gift Bag and Childhood Gift Bag
Instructions are on page 136.

Holiday Memories Gift Bag
Childhood Gift Bag

Anyone receiving these presents will know you were thinking only of them! Fabric and scrapbook papers dress the packages with plenty of personality.

Fabric-Covered Canister
- fabric (we used a 10$\frac{1}{2}$"x22$\frac{1}{4}$" piece)
- decoupage glue
- disposable foam brush
- canister (ours is 6$\frac{1}{2}$" dia.x10$\frac{1}{8}$" tall)
- red and green wool roving
- felting needle tool and mat
- three 1" dia. foam balls
- tissue paper
- green wool felt scraps
- green and red embroidery floss
- fabric glue
- 1$\frac{1}{2}$"w twill tape (we used a 36" length)
- hook-and-loop fastener

Read Needle Felting on page 141 before beginning.

1. Press the fabric edges $\frac{3}{4}$" to the wrong side. Overlapping the edges at the back, use decoupage glue and cover the canister with the fabric, allowing room for the lid. Brush decoupage glue over the fabric.
2. To make each berry, place strips of red roving across the felting needle mat and cross them with more strips. *Needle Felt* the strips together, adding roving as needed to make the felted piece large enough to wrap around a foam ball.

Needle Felt one corner of the felted piece to the foam ball. Wrap the piece around the ball, *Needle Felting* until the ball is covered. Trim away any extra roving and *Needle Felt* to blend in the cut edges.
3. To make each small leaf, place strips of green roving across the felting needle mat and cross them with more strips. *Needle Felt* the strips together, adding roving as needed to make the felted piece a little larger than the small leaf pattern on page 156. Pin the small leaf pattern cut from tissue paper to the felted roving and cut out.
4. Use the pattern and cut 2 large leaves from wool felt. Use 6 strands of green floss to *Blanket Stitch* (page 142) each small leaf to the center of a large leaf and add *Running Stitches* for the veins. Overlapping the stem ends, glue the leaves to a piece of wool felt and cut out.
5. Thread a length of red floss through the leaves, then through a berry from bottom to top. Thread the floss back through the berry and leaves and knot the ends at the back. Repeat to sew the remaining berries to the leaves.
6. Glue each end of a twill tape length 1" to the wrong side. Glue half of the fastener to each end and the leaves to one end of the tape. Fasten the tape around the canister.

Pom-Pom Package and Pinwheel Package
Instructions are on pages 136-137.

Fabric-Covered Canister
Pom-Pom Package
Pinwheel Package

Vintage Linen Wrap

This clever wrap is just right for a small gift like a stationery set, book or journal. Fold the bottom, then side points of a linen napkin to the center, overlapping the points to form an envelope. Tack the bottom and side points together and fold the top point down. For the closure, make a layered scrapbook paper and cardstock tag and add a definition sticker. Thread ribbon or a strip cut from a tablecloth, towel or napkin through slits cut in the tag and attach the closure to the wrap with brads.

Vintage Linen Wrap
Gift Tags

Bottle Sleeve

Gift Tags
(shown on page 68)

For quick & easy gift tags, use a die-cutting tool to cut tags from cardstock or scrapbook paper (ours are 4³/₄" tall). Zigzag a motif cut from Christmas fabric onto a tag and add a chipboard word. Or sew along the center of the tag to attach layered ribbon and trim scraps, and then sew buttons to the tag. Tie twill tape through the hole in each tag.

Bottle Sleeve
Read Felting on page 141 before beginning.

Wrap a favorite bottled beverage in style! Cut a sleeve from a felted wool sweater slightly longer than the bottle. Cut a circle from the sweater the same size as the cut end of the sleeve. Matching right sides, zigzag the circle to the cut sleeve end; turn right side out. For the tie, cut a border from a vintage tablecloth or napkin. Press the long edges to the center back and zigzag with clear thread. Place the bottle in the sleeve and close with the tie.

For the tag, cut a 3¹/₂" diameter circle each from cardstock and scrapbook paper. Pink the edge of the paper circle; then, glue the circles together. Tie ribbon through a hole punched in the tag. Adhere a chipboard Christmas tree to the tag with adhesive foam dots and tie the tag onto the bottle sleeve tie.

69

Want to give a gift that gives (at least) twice? Fabric Package Wraps are fast to finish, and each can be reused! Just think of all the possibilities… storing silverware or linens, securing jewelry for travel or keeping photo albums dust-free, just to name a few!

Package Wraps
Instructions are on page 137.

Package Wraps

Package Wraps

OH · SO · Good Gifts from the Kitchen

Yummy gifts from the kitchen are always the perfect fit! Make Rosemary-Flavored Oil for your favorite cook or Chocolate-Peppermint Bark for everyone at the office. The Country Friends have gathered over a dozen tasteful recipes for sharing, and they've put together wonderful ways to present each one. A White Chocolate Chip Cheese Ball will satisfy a sweet tooth, while Sesame-Parmesan Rounds are just right for savory snacking. Clear off the countertops and get out the mixing bowls…you're about to stir up the best kind of Christmas fun!

Rosemary-Flavored Oil
Flavored Oil Set

Rosemary-Flavored Oil

This is a great way to use the rosemary growing in your garden.

1 c. olive oil
1 t. fresh rosemary leaves, minced
4 fresh rosemary sprigs

Combine oil and minced rosemary in a glass container. Cover and allow to sit for 8 hours.

Strain and discard rosemary. Place rosemary sprigs in a decorative bottle with a lid and add flavored oil. Store in refrigerator up to 10 days. Makes one cup.

Flavored Oil Set instructions begin on page 137.

Chocolate-Peppermint Bark

A wonderful blend of flavors!

$1/4$ c. almonds, finely chopped
8-oz. pkg. semi-sweet baking
    chocolate squares, chopped
6-oz. pkg. white baking chocolate
    squares, chopped
$1/2$ t. peppermint extract
red food coloring
$1/3$ c. peppermint candies, crushed

    Line an 8"x8" baking pan with
aluminum foil. Spread almonds in
pan; set aside. Place semi-sweet
chocolate in a microwave-safe
bowl. Microwave on high setting
for one minute; stir until smooth.
Microwave an additional 10 to
15 seconds, if needed. Pour semi-
sweet chocolate over almonds.
Allow to harden.

    Repeat microwave melting
instructions for white chocolate.
Stir peppermint extract into white
chocolate. Pour half of chocolate
into another bowl and tint pink.
Slowly pour white and pink
chocolate over semi-sweet
chocolate; gently swirl with a knife.
Sprinkle top with crushed candies.
Chill until firm, about one hour.

    Use foil to lift candy from pan;
break into pieces. Store tightly
covered at room temperature.
Makes about one pound.

Peppermint Package, Pizzelle Cone
and Toffee Box instructions are on
page 138.

Pizzelles

*Thin, wafer-like cookies with an
anise taste.*

6 eggs, beaten
$1^1/2$ c. sugar
1 c. butter, melted and cooled
2 T. anise extract
$3^1/2$ c. all-purpose flour
4 t. baking powder

    Place eggs in a bowl; gradually
beat in sugar until smooth. Add
butter and anise extract; mix well.
Combine flour and baking powder;
gradually stir into egg mixture. Drop
rounded teaspoonfuls of dough onto
a heated pizzelle iron. (We used an
iron that makes two 5-inch diameter
pizzelles.) Bake according to
manufacturer's instructions. Quickly
roll each pizzelle into a cone shape
and use a wooden skewer to make a
hole in each side of cone to attach
ribbon hanger. Makes 3 dozen.

Vickie

**Pizzelle
Pizzelle Cone**

**Chocolate-Peppermint Bark
Peppermint Package**

Easy Microwave Butter Toffee
Toffee Box

Easy Microwave Butter Toffee

I love to wrap up this toffee & place it in a special container to share with family and friends. It's so quick & easy!

1¹/₃ c. sugar
1 c. butter
2 T. water
1 T. dark corn syrup
1 t. vanilla extract
³/₄ c. semi-sweet chocolate chips
²/₃ c. chopped walnuts

Line a 13"x9" baking pan with ungreased aluminum foil; set aside.

Place sugar, butter, water, and corn syrup in a large microwave-safe bowl. Microwave on high setting for 4 minutes; stir. Heat an additional 6 to 8 minutes, stirring every 2 minutes, until thickened and golden. Add vanilla; stir well. Pour into prepared baking pan. Sprinkle chocolate chips over top; spread melted chocolate. Sprinkle with walnuts. Let cool completely; break into pieces. Makes about one pound.

Sherri Fisher
Wichita, KS

Banana-Nut Muffins

A welcome breakfast treat.

1 c. sugar
1 c. ripe bananas, mashed
2 eggs
$1/4$ c. oil
2 c. biscuit baking mix
$1/2$ c. chopped pecans
$1/2$ c. brown sugar, packed

Mix sugar, bananas, eggs and oil together. Stir in biscuit baking mix and pecans. Fill paper-lined muffin cups $2/3$ full. Sprinkle brown sugar over tops. Bake at 350 degrees for 25 to 30 minutes. Makes one dozen.

Tea Gift Set

- single server teapot with cup (ours is $4^1/2$" dia.x$7^1/2$" tall)
- tracing paper
- graphite transfer paper
- scrapbook paper
- wavy-edged scissors
- rub-on holiday message
- 4"x6" plastic zipping bag filled with Mint Tea Mix
- $1/4$" dia. hole punch
- $3/8$"w velveteen ribbon
- tea infuser

Find a single server teapot at your local do-it-yourself pottery studio. Take the traced patterns from page 154 or your own drawn pattern and a piece of graphite paper to the studio to transfer the designs. The shop will provide everything you need to complete your teapot set.

For the tea bag topper, fold a $4^1/2$" scrapbook paper square in half. Trim the bottom edges with the wavy scissors and apply the rub-on to the front. Place the topper on the bag and punch 2 holes, 1" apart, through the topper and the bag above the zipper. Thread ribbon through the holes and knot the ends at the front. Tie ribbon around the center of the infuser and attach the infuser to the knot on the topper.

**Banana-Nut Muffin
Muffin Box**

Muffin Box

Place a Banana-Nut Muffin in a custard cup inside a clear plastic cube lined with scrapbook paper (ours is 4"). Tie ribbon around the cube and add a scrapbook paper tag with a rub-on message.

Mint Tea Mix

Your tea-drinking friends will welcome this gift!

1½ c. loose tea leaves
.25-oz. jar dried mint leaves
2 T. dried orange peel
2 T. whole cloves

Combine all ingredients and store in an airtight container. Give with instructions to serve.

Instructions: For one cup of tea, place one teaspoon tea mix in an individual infuser. Pour one cup boiling water over infuser. Allow tea to steep 3 to 5 minutes. Remove infuser; serve hot.

For one quart of tea, place 2 tablespoons tea mix in a teapot. Pour one quart boiling water over tea mix. Allow tea to steep 3 to 5 minutes. Strain tea; serve hot.

Mint Tea Mix
Tea Gift Set

White Chocolate Chip Cheese Ball
Cheese Ball Plate

White Chocolate Chip Cheese Ball

A sweet treat to the very last bite!

8-oz. pkg. cream cheese, softened
1/2 c. butter, softened
1/2 t. almond extract
3/4 c. powdered sugar
1 c. white chocolate chips
1/2 c. sweetened, dried cherries, chopped
3/4 c. sliced almonds, lightly toasted
Garnish: white chocolate curls and sweetened, dried cherries

Beat together cream cheese, butter and almond extract until fluffy. Gradually beat in powdered sugar. Stir in chocolate chips and 1/2 cup cherries. Cover and refrigerate until firm enough to handle, about 2 hours.

Place cream cheese mixture on plastic wrap and shape into a ball. Refrigerate until ready to serve or at least one hour. Roll ball in almonds before serving. Garnish top with white chocolate curls and dried cherries, if desired. Serve with graham cracker snack sticks. Makes about 2 cups.

Sesame-Parmesan Rounds

These crispy cheese-flavored crackers will be one of your favorite recipes!

2 c. all-purpose flour
1/2 t. ground red pepper
1/8 t. salt
1 c. butter, softened
1 c. grated Parmesan cheese
1 egg white
1 t. water
1/4 c. sesame seed, lightly toasted

Combine flour, red pepper and salt; set aside. In a separate bowl, beat butter and cheese until well blended. Add dry ingredients to creamed mixture; stir until well blended. On a lightly floured surface, use a floured rolling pin to roll out dough to 1/8-inch thickness. Use a 2 1/2-inch diameter scalloped-edge cookie cutter to cut out crackers. Place on a greased baking sheet. In a small bowl, whisk together egg white and water. Brush dough with egg white mixture and sprinkle with sesame seed. Bake at 350 degrees for 10 to 12 minutes. Store in an airtight container. Makes about 4 dozen.

Cheese Ball Plate and Lunch Box instructions are on page 139.

Sesame-Parmesan Rounds
Lunch Box

79

Laurie's Special Sugar Cookies

My love of baking came from making delicious cookie creations with my grandma.

2 c. all-purpose flour
1 1/2 t. baking powder
1/4 t. salt
1/4 c. plus 2 T. butter, softened
1/3 c. shortening
3/4 c. sugar
1 egg
1 T. milk
1 t. vanilla extract
green and red food coloring

Combine flour, baking powder and salt; set aside. Beat butter and shortening with an electric mixer until soft; add sugar and beat until fluffy. Add egg, milk and vanilla; beat well. Gradually add flour mixture and mix until blended. Divide dough in half; tint one half green and remaining half red. Cover and chill for 2 hours.

Roll green dough out to 1/8-inch thickness on a lightly floured surface. Cut dough with a floured 2 1/2-inch diameter round cookie cutter; arrange cookies on greased baking sheets. Use a drinking straw to make a hole in the center of each cookie. Bake at 375 degrees for 7 to 8 minutes until just golden around the edges. Repeat with red dough using a floured 2 1/2-inch wide star-shaped cookie cutter. Cool completely on wire racks. Makes about 5 dozen.

Laurie Costa
Maxwell, CA

Laurie's Special Sugar Cookies
Cookie Tassel

Homemade Strawberry Jam

Our family's favorite jam...we also heat it up and pour it over ice cream.

5 c. strawberries, hulled and crushed
1 3/4-oz. pkg. powdered pectin
7 c. sugar
8 half-pint canning jars and lids, sterilized

Combine strawberries and pectin in an 8-quart heavy saucepan; bring to a rolling boil over high heat, stirring constantly. Mix in sugar; return to rolling boil and boil for one minute. Skim off and discard any foam. Ladle into jars, leaving 1/8-inch headspace; wipe rims and secure lids. Process in a boiling water bath for 10 minutes; set jars on towels to cool. Check to make sure lids are sealed. Makes 8 half-pints.

Carol Burns
Delaware, OH

Homemade Strawberry Jam
Jar Topper

Grandma's Date-Nut Bread

This is my favorite recipe for two good reasons...it's simple to make and tastes great!

1 c. boiling water
1/2 c. chopped dates
1 t. baking soda
1 c. brown sugar, packed
1 egg
1 1/4 c. all-purpose flour
1 c. nuts, chopped
1 t. vanilla extract

In a large bowl, combine boiling water, chopped dates and baking soda; set aside.

Beat together brown sugar and egg for about 2 minutes in a separate mixing bowl; add to date mixture. Stir in flour, nuts and vanilla; pour into 3 greased and floured 6"x3" loaf pans. Bake at 350 degrees for 30 to 35 minutes or until wooden pick inserted in center comes out clean; leave in pans 5 minutes. Turn out on a wire rack to cool. Makes 3 loaves.

Sue Wrobel
LaCrosse, WI

Cookie Tassel, Jar Topper and Cutting Board instructions are on pages 139-140.

Grandma's Date-Nut Bread Cutting Board

Coconut-Oatmeal Cookies

A really different, crunchy-chewy coconut-lover's treat!

$1/2$ c. all-purpose flour
$1/2$ t. baking soda
$1/2$ t. baking powder
$1/2$ t. salt
$1/2$ c. butter, softened
$1/2$ c. sugar
$1/2$ c. brown sugar, packed
1 egg
1 t. vanilla extract
1 c. shredded coconut
1 c. quick-cooking oats,
    uncooked
1 c. sweetened, dried
    cranberries
$1/2$ c. almonds, chopped
5 oz. white melting chocolate

Combine flour, baking soda, baking powder and salt. In a separate bowl, beat butter and sugars until fluffy. Beat in egg and vanilla. Add flour mixture to butter mixture. Stir in coconut, oats, cranberries and almonds. Drop by tablespoonfuls 3 inches apart onto greased baking sheets. Bake at 350 degrees for 10 to 12 minutes or until bottoms are golden. Place cookies on wire racks to cool.

Melt white chocolate in the microwave in a glass measuring cup. Dip half of each cookie into chocolate; place on wire racks and allow chocolate to harden. Makes about 5 dozen.

Coconut-Oatmeal Cookies
Cookie Jar

Cookie Jar

- pinking shears
- scrapbook papers
- glass canning jar (ours is $4^{1}/_{4}$" dia.x$9^{1}/_{2}$"h with a $3^{1}/_{4}$" dia. mouth)
- stapler
- $1^{1}/_{2}$"w and $1/_{8}$"w ribbons
- Coconut-Oatmeal Cookies
- fine-point permanent pen
- textured cardstock
- craft glue
- chipboard frame

For the ribbon cookie lift, use the pinking shears to cut a scrapbook paper circle to fit in the jar. Staple the circle to the center of a length of $1^{1}/_{2}$" ribbon. Place the circle at the inside bottom of the jar, letting the ribbon ends hang over the jar sides on the outside. Fill the jar, alternating cookies and pinked scrapbook paper circles. Place the flat lid on the jar. Knot the ribbon ends and twist the screw ring onto the jar; trim the ribbon ends. Write a message on cardstock and glue it to the back of the frame. Tie the frame around the jar with $1/_{8}$" ribbon.

Spiced Applesauce Cakes

Fresh-from-the-orchard taste in individual-size cakes. Serve on mini cake stands with glass dome lids. Personalize twill tape with rub-on letters and tie to the lids, tucking in berry sprigs.

$1/3$ c. butter, softened
$1^1/3$ c. sugar
2 eggs
1 c. applesauce
$1/3$ c. water
$1^2/3$ c. all-purpose flour
1 t. baking soda
$3/4$ t. salt
$1/2$ t. cinnamon
$1/2$ t. ground cloves
$1/4$ t. ground ginger
$1/4$ t. baking powder
$1/2$ c. walnuts, finely chopped
Garnish: $1^1/2$-inch and 2-inch wide
    star-shaped sugar cookies
    (made from purchased
    refrigerated cookie dough)

Beat butter and sugar together; beat in eggs, one at a time, until mixture is light and fluffy. Add applesauce and water; set aside.

In another bowl, combine next 7 ingredients; blend into applesauce mixture. Fold in walnuts. Pour into a greased and floured 6-mold Bundt® pan (each mold holds one cup). Bake at 350 degrees for 20 to 25 minutes or until a toothpick inserted in cakes comes out clean. Cool in pan 10 minutes; remove cakes from pan and cool on a wire rack. Place cakes on serving plates or mini cake stands and drizzle with Caramel Sauce. Garnish with sugar cookies, if desired. Makes six 4-inch diameter cakes.

Spiced Applesauce Cakes

Caramel Sauce

Tastes great on spice cake, pound cake, shortbread and ice cream.

1 c. brown sugar, packed
$1/2$ c. whipping cream
$1/4$ c. corn syrup
1 T. butter
2 t. cinnamon

In a large saucepan, heat all ingredients to boiling, stirring constantly. Reduce heat and simmer, uncovered, for about 5 minutes. Makes $1^1/2$ cups.

Chocolate Torte
Cake Stand

Chocolate Torte

For prettier chocolate layers, use cocoa instead of flour in the greased cake pans.

18.25 oz. pkg. devil's food
    cake mix
2 12-oz. pkgs. white chocolate
    chips
1 c. whipping cream
$2/3$ c. seedless raspberry jam
Garnish: dark chocolate curls,
    fresh raspberries, artificial
    holly leaves

Mix cake according to package directions. Grease three 9" round cake pans and sprinkle with cocoa. Pour batter into prepared pans. Bake at 350 degrees for 15 to 17 minutes or until a wooden pick inserted in center comes out clean. Cool in pans 5 minutes; remove from pans and cool completely on wire racks.

For frosting, cook white chocolate chips and cream over low heat until chocolate melts, stirring often. Chill 45 minutes or until thickened, stirring occasionally. Returning mixture to refrigerator after beating, beat mixture with electric mixer 5 minutes at 15-minute intervals until mixture is thick enough to spread.

Place one cake layer on a serving plate. Spread $1/3$ cup jam on layer and $1/3$ of the frosting; repeat with second layer. Place remaining layer on top and spread remaining frosting on top. Garnish with chocolate curls, raspberries and holly leaves, if desired. Makes 16 servings.

Cake Stand

Cut 4 ribbon lengths long enough to drape over your cake stand with the ends $3/4$" above the table. Press, then glue or fuse the corners of each ribbon end to the wrong side to form a point. Sew a jingle bell to each point. Arrange the ribbons and fresh greenery on the cake stand and place the Chocolate Torte on a serving plate on top.

Christmas Tree Favors

- tracing paper
- scrapbook papers
- craft knife and cutting mat
- craft glue
- glitter
- double-stick tape
- Marvelous Mocha Fudge
- parchment paper
- $1/2$" star punch
- toothpicks

1. For each favor, use the pattern on page 157 and cut a scrapbook paper box. Use the craft knife to cut a slit along the solid gray line. Add glitter to the tree as desired.
2. Fold the box along the dashed lines and tape the bottom sections together. Place a piece of fudge inside the box on a parchment paper piece and tuck the tab in the slit.
3. Punch 2 scrapbook paper stars; add glitter to the stars and glue them together with a toothpick in between. Insert the toothpick in the top of the tree.

Marvelous Mocha Fudge Christmas Tree Favors

Marvelous Mocha Fudge

One piece of this rich fudge goes a long way!

$1^1/2$ c. sugar
$^2/_3$ c. evaporated milk
3 T. instant coffee granules
2 T. butter
$1/4$ t. salt
2 c. mini marshmallows
2 c. semi-sweet chocolate chips
1 t. vanilla extract
$1/2$ t. cinnamon

Combine first 5 ingredients in a heavy saucepan; bring to a full rolling boil over medium heat, stirring constantly. Boil and stir for 3 to 4 minutes; remove from heat. Mix in remaining ingredients; stir until marshmallows are melted. Spread into an 8"x8" baking pan lined with aluminum foil; refrigerate 2 to 3 hours until firm. Lift fudge from pan, remove foil and cut into one-inch pieces. Makes about 4 dozen.

Christmas at Home

Being home for Christmas…a time for settling in by a cozy fire, listening to Christmas music and enjoying a special time together. Old-fashioned favorites like pecan-topped Sweet Potato Casserole, savory Farmhouse Dressing and Turkey Breast with Vegetables pair up perfectly with tangy Frozen Cranberry Salad. Make it a special time together…play games, giggle over well-kept secrets and count down to the big day!

Janet's Shrimp Ball

No special occasion or celebration goes by without someone requesting this appetizer.

8-oz. pkg. cream cheese, softened
4¹/₂-oz. can salad shrimp, drained
1¹/₂ t. onion, minced
1 t. seasoned salt flavor enhancer
¹/₂ t. lemon juice
1 c. chopped pecans

Mix together first 5 ingredients and form a ball. Roll in pecans until covered. Serve with assorted crackers. Serves 10 to 12.

Janet Catt
Camano Island, WA

Festive Holiday Spread

Arrange crackers around this tasty spread and watch it disappear!

CURL UP & GET COZY

8-oz. pkg. cream cheese, softened
1 bunch green onions, chopped
4¹/₂-oz. can chopped green chiles
4-oz. can chopped black olives
16-oz. container sour cream
1 tomato, finely chopped

Blend together cream cheese, onions, chiles and olives. Place cream cheese mixture on a serving platter and form into a candy cane shape. Cover with plastic wrap and chill.

Remove plastic wrap from spread 15 minutes before serving. Spread sour cream over mixture. Arrange tomatoes over sour cream to form stripes. Serve with assorted crackers. Makes 10 to 12 servings.

Bea Hegarty
Gilbert, AZ

Festive Holiday Spread

Frozen Cranberry Salad

Spoon into muffin cups or individual serving dishes and freeze.

2 3-oz. pkgs. cream cheese,
   softened
8-oz. can crushed pineapple
2 T. mayonnaise
2 T. sugar
16-oz. can whole cranberry sauce
1/2 c. chopped pecans
1 c. frozen whipped topping, thawed
Garnish: chopped pecans

Blend cream cheese until fluffy; mix in pineapple, mayonnaise and sugar. Fold in cranberry sauce and 1/2 cup pecans; stir in whipped topping. Spoon into muffin cups or ramekins. Cover with plastic wrap and freeze. Thaw slightly before serving; garnish with chopped pecans, if desired. Makes 6 to 8 servings.

Sue Dunlap
Huntsville, AL

Round-Up Green Beans

Make a day or two ahead of time and store in the fridge until ready to serve.

1 c. catsup
1 c. brown sugar, packed
1 T. Worcestershire sauce
4 14 1/2-oz. cans green beans,
   drained
6 slices bacon, diced
1 onion, chopped
salt and pepper to taste

Combine first three ingredients; toss with green beans and set aside. Sauté bacon and onion until bacon is crisp; drain and add to beans. Salt and pepper to taste; pour into a greased 2-quart baking dish. Cover and bake at 325 degrees for one hour or until heated through. Makes 12 to 16 servings.

Lucinda Lewis
Brownstown, IN

Frozen Cranberry Salad

Sweet Potato Casserole

My grandmother always made this for our family and now, my mom makes this yummy dish for holidays.

3 c. canned sweet potatoes,
   drained and mashed
8-oz. can crushed pineapple
1 c. sugar
1 c. milk
1/2 c. chopped pecans
2 eggs
1 c. brown sugar, packed
1 c. whole pecans
1/2 c. butter
1/2 c. all-purpose flour

Mix first 6 ingredients together; spread into a greased 2-quart baking pan and set aside. Combine remaining ingredients in a saucepan; heat over low heat until butter is melted and sugar is dissolved. Pour over sweet potato mixture; bake, uncovered, at 350 degrees for 30 minutes. Makes 8 to 10 servings.

Paula Eggleston
Knoxville, TN

Wild Rice Soup

I make a double batch of this soup every Christmas. Our family...13 children and spouses, 29 grandchildren and one great-grandchild always gather at my in-laws' home for Christmas. There's usually none left to bring home!

1/2 c. wild rice
1 lb. bacon
1 c. onion, chopped
3/4 c. celery, chopped
1/3 c. green pepper, chopped
2 14-oz. cans chicken broth
2 10-oz. cans cream of mushroom soup
4-oz. can sliced mushrooms
1 pt. half-and-half

Wash wild rice thoroughly; then, boil for 15 minutes. Drain, rinse and set aside.

Cut bacon into 2-inch pieces and fry until crisp in a large Dutch oven. Remove bacon from pan and discard all but 3 tablespoons of drippings. Sauté onion, celery and green pepper in bacon drippings until onion is transparent. Add rice, broth, soup, mushrooms and bacon. Cover and cook over low heat for one hour. Before serving, pour in half-and-half and heat. Makes 10 cups.

Merrill Sakry
Becker, MN

Rosemary Twists

Scrumptious when served with savory soups and stews.

1/3 c. butter, melted
1 t. dried rosemary
1/2 t. garlic, minced
2 1/4 c. all-purpose flour
2 T. grated Parmesan cheese
3 1/2 t. baking powder
1 T. sugar
1/2 t. salt
1 c. milk

Combine butter, rosemary and garlic in a 13"x9" baking pan; tilt to coat bottom of pan. Combine flour, cheese, baking powder, sugar and salt in a mixing bowl; stir in milk until just moistened. Turn dough onto a lightly floured surface; knead 10 times or until smooth. Roll dough into a 12x6-inch rectangle; cut into 12, one-inch wide strips. Place in pan and turn to coat with butter mixture. Twist each strip about 6 times. Arrange strips 2 inches apart on a greased baking sheet and bake at 425 degrees for 20 to 25 minutes or until golden. Makes one dozen.

Gail Prather
Lakeside, CA

Wild Rice Soup
Rosemary Twists

Turkey Breast with Vegetables

This dish makes its own delicious thick gravy. The recipe works well with other meats, too.

2 to 3 T. oil
6 to 8-lb. skinless turkey breast
1 T. salt
1/2 t. pepper
6 potatoes, peeled and quartered
6 to 8 carrots, peeled and halved
3 turnips, peeled and quartered
2 stalks celery, quartered
2 onions, halved
1/2 head cabbage, quartered
2 0.87-oz. pkgs. brown gravy mix
1-oz. pkg. onion soup mix
2 1/4 c. water

Heat oil in a roasting pan; add turkey breast and sauté on all sides until golden. Sprinkle with salt and pepper. Add vegetables to pan; set aside.

Combine gravy and soup mixes with water; pour over turkey and vegetables. Cover and bake at 350 degrees for 2 to 3 hours, basting with pan juices after 1 1/2 hours. Cook until breast juices run clear when pierced with a fork. Serves 8 to 10.

Tina Stidam
Delaware, OH

Farmhouse Dressing

Using the slow cooker frees up your oven for other baking.

1 c. butter
2 c. celery, chopped
2 8-oz. cans sliced
    mushrooms, drained
1 1/2 c. onion, chopped
1/4 c. parsley sprigs, chopped
12 to 13 c. dry bread cubes
1 t. poultry seasoning
1 1/2 t. salt
1 t. sage
1 t. pepper
1/2 t. marjoram
3 to 4 c. chicken broth
2 eggs, lightly beaten

Melt butter in skillet and sauté celery, mushrooms, onion and parsley. In a large bowl, pour mixture over bread cubes. Add seasonings and toss together. Pour in enough broth to moisten. Add eggs; mix well. Lightly pack into a 4-quart slow cooker. Cover and cook on high for 45 minutes; reduce to low and cook for 4 to 8 hours. Makes 12 to 14 servings.

Karen Antonides
Gahanna, OH

Trish's Peanut Butter Pie

Make it extra peanutty...sprinkle with chopped peanuts.

1/2 c. creamy peanut butter
1/2 c. milk
4 oz. cream cheese, softened
8-oz. container frozen whipped
    topping, thawed
9-inch graham cracker crust
Garnish: chopped peanuts

Combine peanut butter, milk and cream cheese in a bowl; blend until smooth. Fold in whipped topping; pour into pie crust. Freeze about 30 minutes; store in the refrigerator. Garnish with chopped peanuts, if desired. Makes 6 to 8 servings.

Trish Gothard
Greenville, KY

Trish's Peanut Butter Pie

Slow Cooker Chocolate Pudding Cake

Warm and chocolatey...yum!

18.25-oz. pkg. chocolate cake mix
3.9-oz. pkg. instant chocolate
    pudding mix
2 c. sour cream
4 eggs
1 c. water
3/4 c. oil
1/4 t. salt
2 c. semi-sweet chocolate chips
non-stick vegetable spray
whipped cream or ice cream

Combine dry cake mix, pudding mix, sour cream, eggs, water, oil and salt in a mixing bowl. Beat on medium speed with an electric mixer for 2 minutes. Stir in chocolate chips. Pour into a slow cooker sprayed with non-stick vegetable spray. Cover and cook on low for 5 hours or until a toothpick comes out with moist crumbs. Serve topped with whipped cream or ice cream. Makes 10 to 12 servings.

Tracie Smith
Bluffton, IN

Slow Cooker Chocolate Pudding Cake

Here Comes SANTA!

When Santa comes to town, it's time for a celebration! The kids can help prepare most of these recipes. They include delicious drinks, yummy appetizers and oh-so-good sweets. Why not make extras and invite the neighbors so everyone can take home a plate of goodies for Santa?

Cranberry Snow Candy

It only takes 3 ingredients to make this yummy candy.

16-oz. pkg. white chocolate chips
1½ c. dried cranberries
1½ c. chopped walnuts

Melt white chocolate chips in the top of a double boiler; remove from heat. Add cranberries and walnuts; drop mixture by teaspoonfuls onto wax paper. Allow to harden. Makes about 2 dozen.

Juanita Williams
Jacksonville, OR

Elf Gorp

A crunchy, baked snack mix that will please all ages!

8 c. popped popcorn
2 c. round crispy oat cereal
2 c. fish-shaped cracker pretzels
2 c. bite-size crispy rice cereal
1 c. peanuts
½ c. butter or margarine, melted
1 T. Worcestershire sauce
½ t. seasoned salt
½ t. garlic powder

Combine first 5 ingredients in a large bowl. Combine butter and remaining ingredients in a small bowl; stir well. Pour over popcorn mixture; toss gently to coat and pour into a large roasting pan. Bake at 250 degrees for one hour, stirring at 15-minute intervals. Cool completely; store in an airtight container. Makes 2½ quarts.

Reindeer Chow

Reindeer Chow

Even young ones can help make this! Pack in pretty jars to have on hand for the holidays or to give as gifts.

4 c. salted peanuts
1 c. whole almonds
1 c. red and green candy-coated chocolate pieces

1 c. raisins
1 c. chopped dates
¼ c. shelled sunflower seeds

Combine all ingredients in a large bowl; store in a covered container. Makes 16 servings.

MaryAnn Nemecek
Springfield, IL

Hearty Cheeseburger Bread

Cut into one-inch wide slices for fun finger food.

2 lbs. ground beef, browned
½ t. garlic powder
¼ c. butter
1 loaf French bread, cut in half
    horizontally
2 c. sour cream
3 c. shredded Cheddar cheese

Combine beef and garlic powder; set aside. Butter both halves of bread; place on an ungreased baking sheet. Stir sour cream into beef mixture; spread onto bread. Sprinkle with cheese. Bake at 350 degrees for 15 to 20 minutes or until cheese melts; slice to serve. Serves 8 to 10.

Marcy Venne
Russell, MA

Taco-Chicken Skewers

Handy skewers make these tasty strips of chicken so easy to eat!

1 c. sour cream
7-oz. jar green salsa
2 T. fresh cilantro, chopped
1¼-oz. pkg. taco seasoning mix,
    divided
4 boneless chicken breast halves, cut
    into 1-inch wide strips
non-stick vegetable spray
Garnish: fresh cilantro leaves

Combine first 3 ingredients and one teaspoon taco seasoning mix in a bowl, stirring well. Cover and chill up to 8 hours, if desired.

Toss chicken with remaining taco seasoning mix. Cook chicken in a large non-stick skillet coated with vegetable spray over medium-high heat 6 to 8 minutes or until done. Serve immediately or cover and chill up to 2 hours. Serve on skewers with salsa mixture. Garnish, if desired. Makes 6 to 8 servings.

Pizza Bites

Refrigerated biscuits make this a quick snack to prepare.

1 c. shredded pizza-blend cheese
½ c. grated Parmesan cheese
10-oz. tube refrigerated flaky biscuits
non-stick vegetable spray
40 slices pre-sliced packaged pepperoni
6 T. plus 2 t. pizza sauce

Combine cheeses; set aside. Cut each biscuit into quarters; roll each quarter into a ball. Use a lightly floured rolling pin to roll each ball into a 2½ to 3-inch circle on a lightly floured surface. Fit circles into miniature muffin cups coated with vegetable spray. Place one pepperoni slice snugly in bottom of each biscuit-lined cup. Spoon ½ teaspoon pizza sauce on top of each pepperoni slice; sprinkle with about 1½ teaspoons of cheese mixture. Bake at 400 degrees for 10 to 12 minutes or until golden. Serve warm. Makes 40.

Pizza Bites

Chocolate Thumbprint Cookies

Chocolate Thumbprint Cookies

A chocolatey twist to an old favorite.

1/2 c. plus 1 t. butter, softened
    and divided
1 c. sugar, divided
1 egg yolk
2 T. plus 2 t. milk, divided
2 1/4 t. vanilla extract, divided
1 c. all-purpose flour
1/3 c. baking cocoa
1/4 t. salt
1/2 c. powdered sugar
24 milk chocolate drops

In a small mixing bowl, beat 1/2 cup butter, 2/3 cup sugar, egg yolk, 2 tablespoons milk and 2 teaspoons vanilla together until light and fluffy; set aside. Combine flour, cocoa and salt; add to butter mixture, beating until well blended. Cover and chill one hour.

Shape dough into one-inch balls. Roll in remaining 1/3 cup sugar; place on lightly greased baking sheets. Press thumb gently into center of each ball. Bake at 350 degrees for 10 to 12 minutes.

While baking, blend together powdered sugar, remaining one teaspoon butter, 2 teaspoons milk and 1/4 teaspoon vanilla. When cookies are done, spoon 1/4 teaspoon filling into each thumbprint; gently press chocolate drop on top of filling. Remove from baking sheets; cool completely on wire rack. Makes 2 dozen.

Ann Fehr
Trappe, PA

Santa's 5-Layer Dip

A ho-ho-ho hit!

8-oz. pkg. cream cheese, softened
1 onion, chopped
2 T. olive oil
16-oz. can refried beans
4 1/2-oz. can chopped green chiles
8-oz. jar taco sauce
8-oz. pkg. shredded Mexican-
    blend cheese

Spread cream cheese in the bottom of an ungreased 13"x9" baking pan; set aside. Sauté onion in olive oil in a skillet until tender; stir in refried beans. Spread bean mixture over cream cheese. Layer green chiles and taco sauce over bean mixture; sprinkle cheese over top. Bake at 325 degrees for 15 to 20 minutes or until cheese is melted. Serve with tortilla chips. Makes 15 to 18 servings.

Jackie Goodnight
Elizabethtown, NC

Fresh Apple Bars

Try these with almonds.

1 3/4 c. sugar
1 c. oil
3 eggs
2 c. all-purpose flour
1 t. baking soda
1/2 t. salt
1/2 t. cinnamon
2 c. apples, peeled, cored and
    sliced
1 c. chopped walnuts
powdered sugar

Beat sugar, oil and eggs together. Add dry ingredients. Fold in apples and walnuts; pour into a greased and floured 13"x9" baking pan. Bake at 350 degrees for 45 to 50 minutes. Cool in pan on wire rack. Cut into bars and sprinkle with powdered sugar. Makes about 15.

Frances Cummons
Lakeview, OH

treat time!

Punch in a Pinch
Need a quick drink...here's one that is sure to please!

2 c. orange juice
1 c. lemon juice
1 c. grenadine
2 qts. ginger ale

Stir juices and grenadine together; chill. Pour mixture into a punch bowl and add ginger ale just before serving. Makes 3 quarts.

*Kathy Riggs
Lewistown, ID*

Popcorn Cake
Children of all ages love to make and eat this cake!

20 c. popped popcorn
1¼ c. butter or margarine
10-oz. pkg. marshmallows (about 40)
1 c. candy-coated chocolate mini baking bits
½ c. peanuts

Place popcorn in a large bowl. Melt butter and marshmallows in the top of a double boiler; pour mixture over popcorn. Stir in remaining ingredients; press into a buttered angel food cake pan. Cool; invert cake onto a serving plate and remove pan. Makes 12 to 16 servings.

*Debra Waggoner
Grand Island, NE*

Santa's Slush

Popcorn Cake

Santa's Slush
What a great Christmasy-colored drink!

2 6-oz. cans frozen limeade concentrate, thawed and undiluted
12-oz. can frozen lemonade concentrate, thawed and undiluted
1 c. powdered sugar
7 c. crushed ice
Optional: green food coloring
33.8-oz. bottle club soda, chilled

Combine half each of first 4 ingredients in a blender; add food coloring, if desired. Blend at high speed until slushy. Pour into an 8"x8" pan. Repeat procedure with remaining half of ingredients, pouring mixture into same pan. Cover and freeze until mixture is firm.

Remove from freezer about 30 minutes before serving. Break mixture into chunks with a spoon; transfer to punch bowl. Add club soda; stir until slushy. Makes about 3 quarts.

Soft Sugar Cookies

Oh-so soft...just what a sugar cookie should be.

1 c. shortening
2 c. sugar
2 eggs
2 t. vanilla extract
4 c. all-purpose flour
2 t. baking powder
1 t. baking soda
1 t. salt
1 c. milk
powdered sugar

Beat shortening and sugar until fluffy. Beat in eggs and vanilla; set aside. In a separate bowl, combine next 4 ingredients; add to sugar mixture alternately with milk, beating well. Chill dough 2 hours.

Drop by teaspoonfuls into powdered sugar and roll into balls. Place on greased baking sheets. Bake at 350 degrees for 11 to 13 minutes. Makes about 5 dozen.

Dayna Hale
Galena, OH

Holly & Yule Cookies

These are so easy and fun for the kids to make.

3¹/₂ c. corn flake cereal
24 marshmallows
6 T. butter
¹/₂ t. vanilla extract
green food coloring
Garnish: 9-oz. pkg. red cinnamon
    candies

Place cereal in a medium bowl. Melt marshmallows, butter and vanilla in the top of a double boiler; tint green. Pour mixture over corn flake cereal; stirring until well coated. Drop by teaspoonfuls onto wax paper. Garnish each with cinnamon candies to resemble holly berries. Makes about 1¹/₂ dozen.

Kim McGeorge
Ashley, OH

Fudgy No-Bake Cookies

Add a cupful of nuts in place of (or right along with!) the coconut for added crunch.

1¹/₂ c. sugar
¹/₂ c. baking cocoa
¹/₂ c. milk
¹/₂ c. butter
1 t. vanilla extract
3 c. quick-cooking oats,
    uncooked
1 c. flaked coconut, packed

Bring sugar, baking cocoa, milk and butter to a rolling boil in a heavy saucepan over medium heat; boil one minute. Stir in vanilla, oats and coconut. Drop by rounded teaspoonfuls onto wax paper; let cool until firm. Makes about 4 dozen.

Shirley Pritchett
Pinckneyville, IL

Hot Christmas Punch

Use star-shaped cookie cutters to cut slices of lemon, limes, oranges and kiwi fruit into the shapes of stars; then float them in your holiday punch.

1 qt. grape juice
1 c. orange juice
1 c. pineapple juice
¹/₂ c. lemon juice
1 qt. boiling water
sugar to taste
Optional: cinnamon sticks

Mix juices, water and sugar; heat thoroughly. Serve with cinnamon stick stirrers. Makes about 10¹/₂ cups.

Jo Baker
Litchfield, IL

97

SHOP until you EAT

Or eat until you shop! If you're not planning to hit the early-morning holiday sales, why not host a shopping day brunch for your friends & family? To help you plan a tasty menu, the Country Friends have chosen a flavorful mix of foods and beverages. Perhaps you'd like to serve the early crowd with warm Bacon-Cheddar Cups and Frosty Orange Juice? Later arrivals will enjoy Chicken Salad Croissants and mugs of Hot Molasses Cider as they share their Christmas bargain-hunting tales. When the morning ends, all the shoppers will agree…your brunch was the best deal of the day!

Farm-Fresh Spinach Quiche

Farm-Fresh Spinach Quiche
The bacon adds the perfect flavor to this quiche!

8 slices bacon, crisply cooked, crumbled and divided
9-inch pie crust
2 c. shredded Monterey Jack cheese
10-oz. pkg. frozen chopped spinach, thawed
    and drained
1½ c. milk
3 eggs, beaten
1 T. all-purpose flour

Sprinkle half of crumbled bacon on bottom of pie crust. Mix cheese, spinach, milk, eggs and flour together. Pour over crust. Sprinkle remaining crumbled bacon on top. Bake at 350 degrees for one hour or until center is set. Makes 8 servings.

Margaret Sloan
Westerville, OH

Mom's Muffin Doughnuts

Hot Molasses Cider
Perfect for sipping!

6 whole cloves
2 lemon slices
1 qt. apple cider
1/4 c. molasses
2 1/4-inch long cinnamon stick
2 T. lemon juice

Insert cloves into lemon slices. In a medium saucepan, bring lemon slices, apple cider, molasses and cinnamon stick to a boil. Reduce heat and simmer for 10 minutes. Discard cinnamon stick. Stir in lemon juice; serve immediately. Makes 4 cups.

Rita Morgan
Pueblo, CO

Mom's Muffin Doughnuts

Mom made these for us when we were kids...they always smelled so good and tasted even better!

2 c. all-purpose flour
1 T. baking powder
1/2 t. salt
1/2 t. nutmeg
1/2 c. sugar
1/3 c. shortening
2 eggs
1 t. vanilla extract
3/4 c. milk
1/2 c. chopped walnuts
1/4 c. butter, melted
1/4 c. cinnamon-sugar

Sift first 4 ingredients together; set aside. In a large bowl, beat sugar with shortening and add eggs and vanilla; beat well. Stir in dry ingredients, milk and walnuts. Pour batter into muffin pan lined with paper muffin cups. Bake at 400 degrees for 17 minutes. Let cool slightly. Brush tops with melted butter and sprinkle with cinnamon-sugar. Serve warm. Makes one dozen.

Lori Doss
Apple Valley, CA

Blueberry Coffee Cake

Blueberry Coffee Cake

A very moist coffee cake, bursting with fresh berry flavor!

2 c. all-purpose flour
1 c. sugar
1 c. milk
1/3 c. butter, softened
1 egg
1 T. baking powder
1 t. salt
1 1/2 c. blueberries

Beat all ingredients, except blueberries, in a large bowl on a low speed for 30 seconds. Then beat on a medium speed for 2 minutes, scraping bowl occasionally.

Grease a 13"x9" pan. Spread half the batter in the pan. Sprinkle blueberries over batter; then, top with remaining batter. Add Streusel Topping and bake at 350 degrees for 40 minutes. Cool 10 minutes in pan. Invert cake onto a baking sheet and invert again onto a serving plate. Drizzle with Glaze. Makes 16 servings.

Streusel Topping:
1/2 c. chopped walnuts
1/3 c. brown sugar, packed
1/4 c. all-purpose flour
1/2 t. cinnamon
1 T. butter, softened

Mix all ingredients together until crumbly. Sprinkle on top of coffee cake.

Glaze:
1 c. powdered sugar
2 T. milk
1/4 t. vanilla extract

Combine all ingredients; drizzle over top of coffee cake.

Susan Kennedy
Delaware, OH

Chicken Salad Croissants

Chicken Salad Croissants

Great for a brunch or a casual weekend lunch.

2 c. cooked chicken, cubed
2/3 c. mayonnaise
1/3 c. celery, diced
1/4 c. raisins
1/4 c. sweetened, dried cranberries
1/4 c. slivered almonds
1 T. fresh parsley, minced
1 T. lemon juice
1 t. mustard
1/8 t. pepper
4 to 6 lettuce leaves
4 to 6 croissants, split in half
  horizontally

Combine the first 10 ingredients in a large bowl; mix well. Cover and refrigerate for 2 to 3 hours. Place a lettuce leaf on the bottom half of each croissant; top with about 1/2 cup chicken mixture. Add the top of croissant. Makes 4 to 6 servings.

Arlene Smulski
Lyons, IL

Fruit Trifle Salad

A fresh fruit salad always makes a brunch complete!

6 oranges, peeled and sliced
3 bananas, sliced
3 c. blueberries
2 c. seedless grapes
3 c. strawberries, halved
4-oz. pkg. instant vanilla pudding
1 3/4 c. milk
3/4 c. sour cream
1 t. orange zest

In a large glass bowl, layer all the fruit in order given. Different fruits (except melons) can be substituted. For the topping, combine pudding mix and milk. Beat for one to 2 minutes. Beat in sour cream and orange zest. Serve sauce separately or pour over fruit. Makes about 16 servings.

Mary Tolle
Upland, CA

Tomato-Basil Bisque

A simple, but very tasty soup!

2 10¾-oz. cans tomato soup
14½-oz. can diced tomatoes
2½ c. buttermilk
2 T. fresh basil, chopped or
    2 t. dried basil
¼ t. pepper
Garnish: shredded fresh basil

Cook first 5 ingredients in a 3-quart saucepan over medium heat, stirring often, 6 to 8 minutes or until thoroughly heated. Garnish, if desired; serve immediately or serve chilled. Makes about 7 cups.

Bacon-Cheddar Cups

Perfect for a family or friends breakfast buffet…they'll go fast!

12 slices white bread
1 T. butter
4 slices bacon, crisply cooked
    and crumbled
½ c. whipping cream
1 egg, beaten
½ T. chives
½ T. onion powder
½ c. shredded Cheddar cheese
salt and pepper to taste
Garnish: cherry tomatoes,
    mushrooms

Cut a 3-inch circle from center of each bread slice. Roll out each circle with a rolling pin to flatten slightly. Grease a 12-cup muffin pan with butter. Press one bread circle in each cup. Bake at 350 degrees for 7 minutes. Divide bacon among cups. Combine whipping cream, egg, chives and onion powder; divide among cups. Sprinkle with cheese. Bake at 350 degrees for 12 minutes. Let stand 5 minutes before serving. Garnish with cherry tomatoes or mushrooms. Makes 12 servings.

Laura Fenneman
Lima, OH

Crunchy Tuna Roll-Ups

Another easy-to-make sandwich for your next brunch!

2 6-oz. cans tuna, drained
½ c. sliced water chestnuts,
    chopped
½ c. green onion, chopped
⅓ c. red pepper, chopped
Optional: 4 eggs, hard-boiled,
    peeled and chopped
½ c. mayonnaise
4 8-inch flour tortillas
2 c. romaine lettuce, shredded

Combine all ingredients except tortillas and lettuce; spread tuna mixture on tortillas. Sprinkle with lettuce and roll up each tortilla tightly. Slice in half diagonally; wrap in plastic wrap and refrigerate up to 3 hours. Makes 8 servings.

Sherry Gordon
Arlington Heights, IL

Pecan-Stuffed Deviled Eggs

Top with fresh parsley sprigs and chopped pecans for a festive presentation.

6 eggs, hard-boiled and peeled
¼ c. mayonnaise
1 t. onion, grated
½ t. fresh parsley, chopped
½ t. dry mustard
⅛ t. salt
⅓ c. pecans, coarsely chopped
Garnish: fresh parsley

Cut eggs in half lengthwise and carefully remove yolks. Mash yolks in a small bowl. Stir in mayonnaise and next 4 ingredients; blend well. Stir in pecans. Spoon or pipe yolk mixture evenly into egg-white halves. Garnish, if desired. Makes 6 servings.

Pecan-Stuffed Deviled Eggs

**Cheese and Tomato Muffins
Creamy Pimiento Cheese Soup**

Frosty Orange Juice

My mom always made this for us on special days, like Christmas, snow days or Sunday brunches. It is so refreshing!

1 c. orange juice
1/2 t. vanilla extract
1/4 c. sugar
1/2 c. milk
4 to 5 ice cubes

Blend all ingredients together in a blender. Makes one serving.

*Kara Kimerline
Galion, OH*

Cheese and Tomato Muffins

My family likes these muffins with scrambled eggs and bacon in the morning or with soup at lunch.

2 1/2 c. all-purpose flour
2 T. sugar
1 1/2 t. baking powder
1 t. dried basil
1 t. salt
1/2 t. baking soda
1 c. plum tomatoes, chopped
1/2 c. milk
2 eggs
1/4 c. butter, melted
2 T. catsup
1 T. onion, minced
1 c. shredded Cheddar cheese, divided

Combine first 6 ingredients; set aside. Mix tomatoes, milk, eggs, butter, catsup and onion together; add to dry ingredients. Stir in 1/2 cup cheese. Fill greased or paper-lined muffin cups 3/4 full. Sprinkle evenly with remaining 1/4 cup cheese; bake at 375 degrees about 18 minutes or until golden. Makes 16.

*May Huffman
Gresham, OR*

Creamy Pimiento Cheese Soup

This rich soup has just a little zing from the hot sauce.

1 T. butter
1 onion, chopped
1 stalk celery, chopped
1 sweet potato, peeled and chopped
4 c. milk
1 1/2 c. chicken broth
4-oz. jar sliced pimientos, drained and divided
1 c. shredded sharp Cheddar cheese
3-oz. pkg. cream cheese, cubed
3/4 t. salt
1/4 t. pepper
1/4 t. hot sauce

Melt butter in a large Dutch oven over medium heat. Add onion and celery; sauté 5 minutes or until vegetables are tender. Add chopped sweet potato, milk and chicken broth; bring to a boil, stirring occasionally. Reduce heat and simmer, stirring occasionally, 18 to 20 minutes or until sweet potato is tender. Remove mixture from heat and stir in half of the pimientos. Add Cheddar cheese and remaining ingredients, stirring until cheese melts. Let cool 5 minutes.

Process cheese mixture, in batches, using a handheld blender, blender or food processor until smooth, stopping to scrape down sides. Stir in remaining pimientos before serving. Makes about 7 cups.

simply Soothing

The most popular hot beverages of winter inspired this collection of soothing sweets, desserts and drinks. Whether you're a fan of coffee or chocolatey cocoa, you'll find something indulgent in these recipes. So get out your favorite mugs and dessert plates …it's time to enjoy a holiday treat and a warm cup of happiness!

Coffee-Nut Torte

A delight for any coffee lover!

6 eggs, separated
2 c. sugar
1 t. vanilla extract
1 c. coffee, cold and divided
1 c. walnuts, ground
2 c. all-purpose flour
3 t. baking powder

Stir egg yolks, sugar, vanilla and 1/4 cup coffee together; beat until thick. In a separate mixing bowl, combine walnuts, flour and baking powder together; add to egg mixture alternately with remaining 3/4 cup coffee. Beat egg whites until stiff peaks form; fold into coffee mixture. Pour into 3 greased, round 9" baking pans. Bake at 350 degrees for 25 minutes. Cool, then frost. Makes 16 servings.

Frosting:
3/4 c. brown sugar, packed
4 1/2 T. all-purpose flour
6 T. milk
1 1/2 t. vanilla extract
3/4 t. maple flavoring
1 1/2 c. butter, softened
3 c. powdered sugar

Combine brown sugar, flour and milk in a saucepan. Stir in vanilla and maple flavoring. Cook over medium heat until thickened; cool slightly. In another mixing bowl, beat butter; gradually add powdered sugar, beating well. Add brown sugar mixture; beat until light and fluffy.

Gail Foster
Leavittsburg, OH

Coffee-Nut Torte

105

Coffee Pie

A great make-ahead pie!

1 c. water
1 T. instant coffee granules
1 T. butter or margarine
30 large marshmallows, cut
    into fourths
1 c. whipping cream, whipped
9-inch pie crust
1/2 c. chopped walnuts, toasted
8-oz. container frozen whipped
    topping, thawed
Garnish: chopped chocolate-
    covered coffee beans

Bring water to a boil in a heavy saucepan; add coffee granules, stirring to dissolve. Add butter and marshmallows. Cook over low heat, stirring occasionally, until marshmallows melt. Cool completely. Fold whipped cream into coffee mixture; spoon into baked pie crust. Sprinkle with walnuts. Refrigerate 8 hours or overnight. Spread whipped topping over pie and garnish, if desired. Makes 8 servings.

Old-Fashioned Cocoa

You'll never go back to instant cocoa again!

1/2 c. unsweetened Dutch-
    processed baking cocoa
1/4 c. powdered sugar
1/2 c. half-and-half
4 c. milk
1 t. vanilla extract
Garnish: whipped cream and
    grated chocolate
Optional: cinnamon and nutmeg
    or peppermint extract

In a small saucepan, combine cocoa and sugar; whisk in half-and-half until mixture is smooth. Over low heat, whisk in milk and vanilla; bring to a simmer. Pour into hot mugs and top with whipped cream and grated chocolate, if desired. For variety, add cinnamon and nutmeg before adding milk or use peppermint extract in place of the vanilla. Makes 4 servings.

Shannon Barnhart
Ashley, OH

Mocha-Almond Coffee Mix

Keep a container of this on hand for unexpected holiday guests!

26-oz. can hot cocoa mix
1 c. plus 2 T. decaffeinated instant
    coffee granules
1 1/2 t. vanilla extract
1 t. almond extract

Mix all ingredients in a medium bowl. Store in an airtight container. To serve, add 3 heaping teaspoons of mix to one cup hot water and stir. Makes approximately 50 to 60 servings.

Rachel Burns
Elko, NV

Sweet Dreams Hot Chocolate

This recipe has been handed down through my family for at least 3 generations!

1 c. milk
chocolate syrup to taste
1/4 t. cinnamon
1/2 t. vanilla extract
Garnish: mini marshmallows

Warm milk in a saucepan on low, taking care not to scorch. Stir in chocolate syrup, cinnamon and vanilla with a small whisk or spoon until dissolved, being careful not to beat. Pour into a mug and top with marshmallows. Makes one serving.

Sarah Lundin
Forest Grove, OR

Coffee Pie

Chocolate Cappuccino Cookies

Serve these irresistible cookies with a tall glass of cold milk or a warming latte.

2 c. butter or margarine,
    softened
4 c. brown sugar, packed
4 eggs
$5\frac{1}{2}$ c. all-purpose flour
1 c. baking cocoa
$\frac{1}{4}$ c. instant coffee granules
1 t. baking powder
1 t. baking soda
1 t. salt
10-oz. pkg. cinnamon chips

Beat butter until creamy. Gradually add brown sugar, beating well. Add eggs, beating until blended. Combine flour and next 5 ingredients. Gradually add to butter mixture, beating at low speed just until blended. Stir in cinnamon chips. Drop dough by rounded tablespoonfuls, 2 inches apart, onto lightly greased baking sheets. Bake at 350 degrees for 8 to 10 minutes. Cool on baking sheets 5 minutes. Remove to wire racks to cool completely. Makes 8 dozen.

Butterscotch Coffee Spice Bars

A sweet treat for coffee and conversation!

1 c. brown sugar, packed
$\frac{1}{2}$ c. shortening
1 egg
$\frac{1}{2}$ c. hot water
1 t. instant coffee granules
2 c. all-purpose flour
1 t. baking powder
$\frac{1}{2}$ t. baking soda
$\frac{1}{2}$ t. salt
$\frac{1}{2}$ t. cinnamon
1 c. butterscotch chips
$\frac{1}{2}$ c. chopped nuts

Combine brown sugar, shortening and egg; beat until creamy. Mix hot water and instant coffee; blend into creamed mixture. Stir together flour, baking powder, baking soda, salt and cinnamon; gradually stir into creamed mixture. Add butterscotch chips and nuts; mix well. Spread in greased and floured 13"x9"x2" pan. Bake at 350 degrees for 25 to 30 minutes. Cool; cut into bars. Makes 2 dozen.

Barbara Nicol
Marysville, OH

the CHEER starts Here

Surrounded by dear friends…it's the perfect way to celebrate Christmas. This year, why not spend time visiting one another's homes for a progressive dinner? Simply get together a group of friends and enjoy a meal together. Each course will be served at a different home, so that the party moves from place to place throughout the evening. It's the perfect way to see each home dressed in its holiday best, and each hostess can prepare her favorite recipe to share.

Brie with Caramelized Onions

A yummy combination of flavors.

8-oz. pkg. round Brie cheese
1 onion, chopped
2 T. butter
1/2 c. brown sugar, packed
1/2 c. sweetened, dried cranberries
2 t. white vinegar
1/4 c. pistachios

Place Brie in a greased baking pan; bake at 350 degrees for 10 minutes. Set aside. Sauté onion in butter; add brown sugar, cranberries and vinegar. Heat until mixture begins to caramelize, about 5 minutes. Pour over Brie; sprinkle with pistachios. Serves 8.

Kathleen Richter
Bridgeport, CT

Jo Ann's Sausage-Stuffed Mushrooms

Bet you can't eat just one!

6 oz. ground sweet Italian
    sausage
1 clove garlic, minced
3 T. olive oil
1/4 c. grated Parmesan cheese
2 T. fresh parsley, minced
16 mushrooms, stems removed

Brown sausage and garlic in oil; drain. Stir in Parmesan cheese and parsley. Spoon mixture into mushrooms. Arrange in a 13"x9" baking dish; bake at 350 degrees for 20 minutes. Serve warm. Makes 16.

Jo Ann

Poinsettia Punch

Chill the champagne and juice in the refrigerator before the party; then mix the punch right before serving.

750 ml. bottle champagne or
    nonalcoholic champagne,
    chilled
3 c. cranberry-apple juice drink,
    chilled
1/4 c. frozen white grape juice
    concentrate, thawed
1/4 c. orange liqueur or orange juice

Stir together all ingredients in a 2-quart pitcher. Makes 8 cups.

109

Cranberry-Pecan Salad

All the ingredients blend together to make this one of our favorites.

2 radicchio bunches, torn
1 red leaf lettuce bunch, torn
1 endive bunch, torn
3 pears, thinly sliced
1/2 c. sweetened, dried cranberries
1/4 c. chopped pecans, toasted
1/4 c. Gorgonzola cheese
1/3 c. pear juice
1/4 c. oil
2 T. vinegar
2 T. lemon juice
1 t. red onion, minced
1/2 t. salt
1/2 t. pepper

In a large mixing bowl, combine salad greens. Toss greens with pears, cranberries, pecans and cheese; set aside.

Before serving, whisk together pear juice, oil, vinegar, lemon juice, red onion, salt and pepper; toss with salad. Makes 14 cups.

Megan Brooks
Antioch, TN

Cranberry-Pecan Salad

Roasted Vegetables

Roasted Vegetables

If your parsnips are wide at the root end, cut chunks in half lengthwise for even cooking.

1 1/2 lbs. carrots, peeled and cut into 1 1/2-inch chunks
1 1/2 lbs. parsnips, peeled and cut into 1 1/2-inch chunks
3 T. olive oil
1 T. sugar
1 1/2 t. kosher salt
1/2 t. pepper

Combine all ingredients in a shallow roasting or broiler pan; toss well and spread in a single layer. Roast at 475 degrees for 30 minutes, stirring after 25 minutes. Makes 4 to 6 servings.

HANG PRETTY ORNAMENTS FROM THE CHANDELIER FOR A HOLIDAY SHINE!

Grilled Parmesan Herb Bread

Use fresh Parmesan cheese and grate it right before adding…a little effort that results in a lot of flavor.

1/2 c. butter, softened
1/2 c. grated Parmesan cheese
1 t. dried oregano
1 t. dried parsley
1 t. dried basil
1 loaf Italian bread, sliced
   one-inch thick

Blend together butter, cheese and herbs; spread on one side of bread slices. Arrange slices on boiler pan and broil until golden. Makes one loaf.

Christine Lennon
Tunkhannock, PA

Best Beef Brisket

This brisket is fork-tender and delicious.

1 t. garlic salt
1 t. garlic powder
1 3/4 t. kosher salt
2 t. pepper
2 T. Worcestershire sauce
5 to 6-lb. beef brisket, trimmed
1/3 c. sugar
1 c. barbecue sauce
1 c. Russian salad dressing

Combine first 5 ingredients; rub into beef. Tightly wrap beef in heavy aluminum foil; place in an ungreased 13"x9" baking pan. Bake at 300 degrees for 5 hours. Carefully remove foil from beef; set beef aside.

Measure one cup of broth; discard any remaining broth. Return brisket to baking pan. Mix together one cup broth, sugar, barbecue sauce and salad dressing; pour over brisket. Bake, covered, at 325 degrees for 30 minutes. Uncover and bake 30 minutes more. Serve with sauce. Makes 10 to 12 servings.

Lynda McCormick
Burkburnett, TX

Fontina Grits and Collards

A new twist on collard greens.

3/4 lb. collard greens, washed and
   stems removed
1/4 c. butter or margarine
1 c. sweet onion, finely chopped
2 T. water
1 1/2 c. chicken broth
1 1/4 c. whipping cream
1/2 c. quick-cooking grits, uncooked
1/2 lb. fontina cheese, cut into
   small cubes

On a cutting board, stack collard leaves; roll up lengthwise. Cut 2 lengthwise slits down leaves; cut crosswise into 1/4-inch strips and set aside.

Melt butter over medium heat in a saucepan. Add onion, sauté 3 minutes or until tender. Add collard greens; sprinkle with water and cook, covered, 4 to 5 minutes or until greens are tender.

Combine broth and cream in a large saucepan; bring to a simmer over medium heat. Reduce heat to low; stir in grits and cook, uncovered, 10 minutes. Add cheese; stir until melted. Stir in cooked collard greens. Makes 4 to 6 servings.

Best Beef Brisket

Velvety Cheesecake

Praline Coffee

A great drink with dessert!

3 c. hot brewed coffee
$^3/_4$ c. half-and-half
$^3/_4$ c. brown sugar, packed
2 T. butter or margarine
$^3/_4$ c. praline liqueur or maple
   syrup
Garnish: sweetened whipped
   cream

Heat coffee, half-and-half, brown sugar and butter over medium heat, stirring constantly, until thoroughly heated (do not boil). Remove from heat and stir in liqueur. Garnish with sweetened whipped cream, if desired. Makes about 6 cups.

Velvety Cheesecake

A traditional Christmas holiday dessert!

1 c. graham cracker crumbs
3 T. sugar
3 T. butter, melted
3 8-oz. pkgs. cream cheese,
   softened
$^3/_4$ c. sugar
2 T. all-purpose flour
2 t. vanilla extract
3 eggs
1 c. sour cream
Toppings: chocolate shell sauce
   sprinkled with chopped turtle
   candies, ready-made cream
   cheese frosting sprinkled with
   peppermint candies

Combine graham cracker crumbs, sugar and butter. Press into the bottom of a 9" springform pan. Bake at 325 degrees for 10 minutes; cool.

Beat cream cheese, sugar, flour and vanilla in a mixing bowl until smooth. Add eggs, one at a time, beating just until yellow disappears. Stir in sour cream. Pour batter into cooled crust. Bake at 325 degrees for 45 minutes or until edges are set and center is almost set. Turn off oven. Immediately run a knife around edge of pan, releasing sides. Close oven door and let cheesecake stand in oven for 45 minutes.

Remove from oven; cool completely in pan on a wire rack. Cover and chill 8 hours.

Remove sides of pan; top with desired toppings. Makes 12 to 14 servings.

Gail Hageman
Albion, ME

Praline Coffee

Spiced Hot Cider

A good drink to warm you up!

1 gal. cider
1 c. brown sugar, packed
6-oz. can frozen orange juice
1 cinnamon stick
3 whole cloves
3 whole allspice

Heat all ingredients and simmer. Remove spices before serving. Makes 10 servings.

Sally Borland
Port Gibson, NY

Cinnamon Bread Pudding

To slightly dry out the bread, place slices on paper towels in a single layer for one hour. This is an absolutely fabulous dessert!

21 slices cinnamon bread, slightly dry
1 c. raisins
1 t. cinnamon-sugar
5 c. milk
6 eggs, lightly beaten
2 c. sugar, divided
2 T. cornstarch
1 c. water
1/4 c. butter, cut into pieces
2 t. vanilla extract

Tear bread into bite-size pieces. Combine bread and raisins in a bowl; spread in a greased 13"x9" baking pan. Sprinkle cinnamon-sugar over bread mixture.

Combine milk, eggs and one cup sugar in a bowl; pour over bread mixture, pressing down gently with a fork to coat. Bake at 350 degrees for one hour or until set and golden.

Combine remaining one cup sugar and cornstarch in a medium saucepan. Stir in water and butter. Bring to a boil over medium-low heat; cook until slightly thickened, stirring frequently. Stir in vanilla. Serve sauce with bread pudding. Makes 10 to 12 servings.

Justine Dillon
Charleston, IL

Cinnamon Bread Pudding

"Egg" Nog

This is great and there are no raw eggs to worry about. My kids love it.

3-oz. pkg. vanilla instant pudding
1/3 c. sugar
8 c. milk
2 t. vanilla extract
1/2 to 1 t. nutmeg

In a large bowl, mix first four ingredients until combined. Add desired amount of nutmeg. Serve chilled. Keeps well in refrigerator. Makes about 8 cups.

Paula Zsiray
Logan, UT

Holiday BAKE SALE

If your school, church or club is planning a fund-raiser, a Christmas bake sale may be just the ticket. From Peanut Butter Fudge to Cherry-Almond Bars, these treats are the kind everyone craves around the holidays. Friends and neighbors are sure to know someone who'd love a gift of Blueberry Jam Muffins or Spicy Pumpkin Pies. Remember to make extras for your family!

Sweet Gingers

While they're baking, these cookies fill the house with a warm, spicy aroma that's irresistible.

3/4 c. shortening
1 c. sugar
1/4 c. molasses
1 egg
2 c. all-purpose flour
1 t. baking soda
1 t. ground cloves
1 t. ground ginger
1/4 t. salt

Beat shortening, sugar and molasses until well blended. Beat in egg. In a separate bowl, combine remaining ingredients; add to sugar mixture, mixing well. Roll dough into walnut-size balls; place on ungreased baking sheets and flatten slightly. Bake at 350 degrees for 10 to 12 minutes. Makes 2 dozen.

Joyce Davis
Greeley, CO

Peanut Butter Fudge

We're hooked on this recipe for creamy fudge!

18-oz. jar creamy peanut butter
7-oz. jar marshmallow creme
3 c. sugar
3/4 c. butter
2/3 c. evaporated milk
1 c. salted peanuts, finely
    chopped
1 t. vanilla extract

Place peanut butter and marshmallow creme in a large bowl. Bring sugar, butter and milk to a boil in a heavy saucepan; boil 5 minutes, stirring constantly. Pour hot sugar mixture over peanut butter mixture, stirring until blended. Stir in peanuts and vanilla. Working quickly, pour mixture into an ungreased 13"x9" pan. Chill one hour or until set. Cut into squares. Makes 3 1/2 pounds.

Cheryl Bigony
Piqua, OH

Chocolate-Peanut Butter Squares

Tastes just like the famous candy!

2 1/2 c. powdered sugar
1/2 c. brown sugar, packed
2 c. creamy peanut butter
3/4 c. margarine, divided
1 t. vanilla extract
6-oz. pkg. semi-sweet
    chocolate chips

Combine sugars, peanut butter, 1/2 cup margarine and vanilla; press into an ungreased 13"x9" baking pan. Melt together chocolate chips and remaining 1/4 cup margarine; pour over peanut butter mixture and refrigerate until firm. Cut into squares. Makes 2 dozen.

Vicki Exum
Roanoke Rapids, NC

Chocolate-Peanut Butter Squares

Hazel's Pumpkin Bread

This recipe was passed down to me from my grandmother. Adding candied cherries makes pumpkin bread even more delightful.

1/2 c. chopped pecans
1 2/3 c. all-purpose flour, divided
1 1/4 c. sugar
1 t. baking soda
1/2 t. cinnamon
1/2 t. nutmeg
1/4 t. salt
1 c. canned pumpkin
1/2 c. oil
2 eggs
1/3 c. water
1/2 c. candied cherries, halved

Toss pecans in one tablespoon of flour. Combine remaining flour and next 5 ingredients in a large mixing bowl; set aside. In a separate bowl, mix together pumpkin, oil, eggs and water. Add pumpkin mixture to dry ingredients; mix well. Fold in cherries and pecans. Pour mixture into a greased and floured 9"x5" loaf pan. Bake at 350 degrees for one hour and 14 minutes or until center tests done. Remove from pan; cool completely on a wire rack. Makes 8 to 10 servings.

Angela Stevens
South Point, OH

Cherry-Almond Bars

Apricot Balls

This recipe came from Grandma. My mom, sister and I bake them every year...wonderful and so easy.

2 c. flaked coconut, firmly packed
1 c. dried apricots, chopped
2/3 c. sweetened condensed milk
1/8 t. salt

Combine all ingredients in a large mixing bowl; mix well. Shape into 3/4-inch balls; place on parchment-lined baking sheets. Bake at 325 degrees for 15 minutes or until golden. Makes about 4 dozen.

Kaki Huckstep
Kingsport, TN

Cherry-Almond Bars

Make ahead of time...these bars freeze well.

1 c. shortening
2 c. sugar
3 c. all-purpose flour
4 eggs
1 t. vanilla extract
1 t. almond extract
1 t. salt
21-oz. can cherry pie filling

Blend shortening and sugar together; add next 5 ingredients and mix well. Pour 3/4 of the batter into a greased 15"x10" jellyroll pan; spread cherry pie filling over the top. Dot with remaining batter; bake at 350 degrees for 30 to 35 minutes. Drizzle with Almond Glaze while still warm; cut into bars to serve. Makes about 3 dozen.

Almond Glaze:
1 c. powdered sugar
1/2 t. vanilla extract
1/2 t. almond extract
2 to 3 T. milk

Stir all ingredients together until well blended.

Deb DeYoung
Zeeland, MI

Toffee

Spicy Pumpkin Pies
Always a good bake sale item!

2 15-oz. cans pumpkin
1 c. brown sugar, packed
1 c. sugar
4 eggs
2 T. molasses
1 T. pumpkin pie spice
1/2 t. salt
2 c. milk
2 pie crusts
Optional: sweetened whipped
    cream and pecan halves

Combine first 7 ingredients;
beat with a whisk until smooth.
Gradually add milk to pumpkin
mixture, whisking until well blended.
Pour filling into unbaked pie
crusts. Bake on bottom rack
at 400 degrees for 10 minutes.
Reduce heat to 350 degrees
and bake one hour or until center
is set. Cool completely before
serving. Garnish with sweetened
whipped cream and pecan halves,
if desired. Makes 16 servings.

Blueberry Jam Muffins
You can use any flavor jam or preserves,
but the blueberry and banana tastes
great together!

1 c. all-purpose flour
1/4 c. sugar
3/4 t. baking powder
1/8 t. baking soda
1/8 t. salt
1/2 c. sour cream
1/4 c. butter, melted
1 banana, mashed
1 egg
1/2 t. vanilla extract
1 to 2 T. milk
1/2 c. blueberry jam

Mix dry ingredients together in
a bowl. Stir in next five ingredients.
Add a little milk if batter seems
too thick. Spoon batter into 10 to
12 greased muffin cups, filling
about half full. Drop one teaspoon
of jam into the middle of each
muffin cup. Bake at 400 degrees
for 12 to 15 minutes. Cool slightly
before removing from pan. Makes
10 to 12.

Becca Bransfield
Burns, TN

Toffee
What a treat…great for munching!

1 c. chopped walnuts
1/2 c. butter
3/4 c. brown sugar, packed
1/2 c. semi-sweet chocolate chips

Butter an 8"x8" baking pan;
spread walnuts on the bottom.
In a saucepan, heat butter and
sugar; bring to a boil, stirring
constantly. Cook until mixture
darkens, about 7 minutes;
immediately pour over walnuts.
Sprinkle chocolate chips over the
top; cover with a baking sheet to
hold in heat until chocolate begins
to melt. Spread chocolate over
top. Refrigerate; break into pieces
when cool. Makes about one pound.

Wendy Lee Paffenroth
Pine Island, NY

Best-Ever Chocolate Pound Cake

It's just what the name says!

16-oz. can chocolate syrup
7-oz. milk chocolate candy bar
2 t. vanilla extract
1 c. butter, softened
2 c. sugar
4 eggs
2¹/₂ c. all-purpose flour
¹/₂ t. baking soda
1 c. buttermilk
1 c. chopped pecans

Place chocolate syrup and candy bar in the top of a double boiler; bring water to a boil. Reduce heat to low; cook until candy bar melts, stirring occasionally. Remove from heat and stir in vanilla. Beat butter at medium speed with an electric mixer 2 minutes or until soft and creamy. Gradually add sugar, beating at medium speed 5 to 7 minutes. Add eggs, one at a time, beating just until yellow disappears. Add chocolate mixture, beating until blended. Combine flour and baking soda; add to butter mixture alternately with buttermilk, beginning and ending with flour mixture. Mix at low speed just until blended after each addition. Fold in pecans. Pour batter into a greased and floured 12-cup Bundt® pan or 10" tube pan. Bake at 325 degrees for one hour and 15 minutes; remove from pan and let cool completely on wire rack. Makes 16 servings.

Nut Praline Crunch

Lemon Bread

This bread is moist and the tart glaze gives it even more flavor.

6 T. shortening
1¹/₃ c. sugar, divided
2 eggs, beaten
1 T. lemon zest
1¹/₂ c. all-purpose flour
1 t. baking powder
¹/₂ t. salt
¹/₂ c. milk
3 T. lemon juice

Beat together shortening and one cup sugar. Beat in eggs and lemon zest. In a separate bowl, combine flour, baking powder and salt; add to shortening mixture alternately with milk, beginning and ending with flour mixture. Pour batter into a greased and floured 8"x4" loaf pan. Bake at 325 degrees for 45 minutes or until wooden pick inserted in center comes out clean. Meanwhile, combine lemon juice and remaining ¹/₃ cup sugar in a small microwave-safe bowl. Microwave on high setting for 30 to 45 seconds; stir until sugar dissolves. Pour glaze over hot bread. Let cool completely in pan. Makes 8 servings.

Laurie Murphy
LaPlata, MD

Nut Praline Crunch

A tin of this was given to me and I asked for the recipe. Now, my sons and I make this to sell at bake sales...what a hit!

1 T. butter
1/2 c. brown sugar, packed
1/4 c. light corn syrup
1/4 t. baking soda
1/4 t. vanilla extract
3 2/3 c. toasted oatmeal cereal
    squares
1 1/4 c. bite-size crispy rice cereal
    squares
2 c. mixed nuts

Combine butter, brown sugar and corn syrup in a microwave-safe bowl. Microwave on high for one minute or until butter is melted. Stir in baking soda and vanilla. In a large bowl, combine cereals and nuts; fold in syrup mixture. Spread on an aluminum foil-lined jelly-roll pan. Bake at 200 degrees for one hour, stirring every 20 minutes. Cool completely and store in an airtight container. Makes about 7 cups.

Pamela Bures-Raybon
Edna, TX

Vanilla Drop Cookies

This recipe has been handed down from my great-grandmother. I've already added it to a special book for my daughter who is only 6 years old.

3/4 c. butter, softened
1 1/4 c. sugar
2 eggs, beaten
1 t. vanilla extract
3 c. all-purpose flour
3 t. baking powder
3/4 t. salt
2/3 c. milk

Beat butter and sugar until fluffy. Beat in eggs; add vanilla. In a separate bowl, sift together flour, baking powder and salt; stir in milk. Add flour mixture to butter mixture; blend well. Chill dough for 3 to 4 hours.

Drop by teaspoonfuls onto ungreased baking sheets. Bake at 350 degrees for 6 minutes or until lightly golden. Makes 2 to 3 dozen.

Susan Biffignani
Fenton, MO

Night & Day Cookies

With both white and dark chocolates, they look like night & day, but they're also good enough to eat all night & day!

1 c. butter, softened
1 c. brown sugar, packed
1 c. sugar
2 t. vanilla extract
2/3 c. baking cocoa
2 eggs
1 t. baking soda
2 c. all-purpose flour
2 c. white chocolate chips
2 c. semi-sweet chocolate chips

Beat butter, sugars and vanilla until fluffy; blend in cocoa, eggs and baking soda. Add flour; mix well. Fold in chips; shape dough into 1 1/2-inch balls. Place 3 inches apart on greased baking sheets; bake at 325 degrees for 14 to 16 minutes. Cool on baking sheets for 2 minutes; transfer to wire racks to cool. Makes 3 1/2 dozen.

Elisabeth Macmillan
British Columbia, Canada

Night & Day Cookies

Caroling Invitations

(also shown on page 9)
- craft glue
- scrapbook paper
- cardstock
- glitter
- white vellum
- vellum tape
- $3/8$"w twill tape
- wired pom-pom trim
- $1/4$" dia. hole punch
- $5/8$" dia. jingle bells
- embroidery floss

For each invitation, glue a 6" scrapbook paper square to the center of a $6^1/2$" cardstock square. Add glitter along the paper edges. Use a computer to print the invitation information on vellum and cut into a $5^1/2$" square. Tape the vellum to the center of the scrapbook paper. Add a twill tape and trim hanger through holes punched in the top corners of the invitation. Tie a bell to the hanger with floss.

Wintry Arrangement

(also shown on page 12)
- 20-gauge copper wire
- wire cutters
- fresh greenery
- 2"w ribbon
- duct tape
- washboard
- utility scissors
- protective gloves
- ultra-thin steel sheets
- $1/4$"w copper foil tape
- assorted acrylic paint colors
- paintbrushes
- three $5/8$"x$2^1/4$" dia. yo-yo wood turnings
- hammer
- #9 upholstery nails
- hot glue gun

1. Wire the greenery stems together and add a ribbon bow. Duct tape the wire ends to the top back of the washboard.
2. For the snowflakes, cut one 6" and two 5" diameter steel circles. Cut three 6" and twelve $1^1/4$" copper tape lengths for the 6" snowflake and three 5" and twelve $1^1/8$" lengths for each 5" snowflake.
3. Adhere the long tape strips to each circle for the base of the snowflake; then, add a V to each end with the short strips. Cut out the steel snowflakes slightly larger than the copper snowflakes.

4. Paint the yo-yos (we painted one dark and light blue, one orange and red and one yellow and green). Nail a snowflake to the center of each yo-yo. Hot glue a wire length to the back of 2 yo-yos and wrap the wire ends around the greenery. Hot glue the remaining yo-yo to the top of the washboard.

Mug Cozy

(also shown on page 14)
- mug
- green and white wool felt
- tissue paper
- green and red embroidery floss
- fabric glue
- $1/4$"w red rickrack
- four $3/8$" dia. buttons

1. For the cozy, measure around the mug from one side of the handle to the other. Cut a 3" wide green felt strip the determined measurement. Cut a $2^1/2$" wide white felt strip $1/2$" shorter than the green strip.
2. Alternating ornament shapes, trace the patterns on page 146 onto tissue paper to fit along the center of the white strip. Pin the tissue paper pattern to the strip. Using 3 strands of floss, *Stem Stitch* (page 142) the outlines through the paper. Tear away the paper and add *Cross Stitches, Straight Stitches* and *French Knots* to the strip as you'd like.

3. Glue the white strip to the center of the green strip and glue rickrack along the white felt edges.
4. Use floss to sew a button to each white felt corner. Cut two 8" floss lengths and knot one end of a length around the floss behind each button on one end of the cozy.
5. With the ends at the sides of the handle, wrap the cozy around the mug. Wrap the floss around the buttons opposite each other in a figure-8 pattern above and below the handle.

Winter Warmers
(also shown on pages 10, 11 and 15)
Read Knit on pages 142-144
before beginning.

Finished Sizes:
Scarf: 7"x54" (18 cm x 137 cm)
Hat: 19" (48.5 cm) circumference
Mittens: Adult size

 INTERMEDIATE

Materials
Medium Weight Yarn
   Version A (Cream):
      [3½ ounces, 210 yards
      (100 grams, 192 meters)
      per skein]:
        Full Set - 3 skeins
        Scarf - 2 skeins
        Hat - 1 skein
        Mittens - 1 skein

Version B (Brown):
      [3 ounces, 197 yards
      (85 grams, 180 meters)
      per skein]:
        Full Set - 3 skeins
        Scarf - 2 skeins
        Hat - 1 skein
        Mittens - 1 skein
Straight knitting needles, size 9
   (5.5 mm) **or** size needed
   for gauge (for Scarf only)
16" (40.5 cm) Circular knitting
   needle, size 9 (5.5 mm) **or** size
   needed for gauge (for Hat only)
Double pointed knitting needles,
   size 9 (5.5 mm) (set of 4) (for
   Hat and Mittens only)
Cable needle
Stitch holders (for Mittens only)- 2
Markers
Yarn needle

Gauge: In pattern, 21 sts and
   25 rows = 4" (10 cm)
In Stockinette Stitch, 17 sts =
   4" (10 cm)

Stitch Guide
Cable 6 Back (abbreviated C6B)
(uses next 6 sts)
Slip next 3 sts onto cable needle
and hold at **back** of work, K3
from left needle, then K3 from
cable needle.

Cable 6 Front (abbreviated C6F)
(uses next 6 sts)
Slip next 3 sts onto cable needle
and hold at **front** of work, K3
from left needle, then K3 from
cable needle.

Scarf
With straight needles, cast on
36 sts.

Row 1: K3, P2, (K1, P2) 4 times, K2,
P2, (K1, P2) 4 times, K3.

Row 2 (Right side): K5, (P1, K2)
4 times, P2, (K2, P1) 4 times, K5.

Rows 3-7: Repeat Rows 1 and 2
twice, then repeat Row 1
once **more**.

Row 8: Knit across.

Row 9: K3, (P2, K1) 3 times, P 12,
(K1, P2) 3 times, K3.

Row 10: K 12, C6B, C6F, K 12.

Row 11: K3, (P2, K1) 3 times, P 12,
(K1, P2) 3 times, K3.

Rows 12-15: Repeat Rows 8
and 9, twice.

(continued on page 122)

Repeat Rows 10-15 for pattern until Scarf measures approximately 52³/₄" (134 cm) from cast on edge, ending by working Row 12.

Last 7 Rows: Repeat Rows 1-7.

Bind off all sts in pattern.

Hat
BODY
With circular needle, cast on 100 sts.

Place a marker to mark the beginning of the round (see Markers, page 143).

Rnds 1-8: K2, P1, K2, P2, K2, (P1, K2) twice, P2, ★ K2, (P1, K2) twice, P2, K2, (P1, K2) twice, P2; repeat from ★ around to last 3 sts, K2, P1.

Rnd 9: ★ K 12, P1, K2, P2, K2, P1; repeat from ★ around.

Rnd 10: ★ C6B, C6F, K8; repeat from ★ around.

Rnd 11: ★ K 12, P1, K2, P2, K2, P1; repeat from ★ around.

Rnd 12: Knit around.

Rnd 13: ★ K 12, P1, K2, P2, K2, P1; repeat from ★ around.

Rnd 14: Knit around.

Repeat Rnds 9-14 for pattern until Hat measures approximately 5¹/₂" (14 cm) from cast on edge, ending by working Rnd 11.

CROWN SHAPING
Note: Change to double pointed needles when necessary.

Rnd 1: ★ K 12, SSK (Figs. 4a-4c, page 143), K4, K2 tog (Fig. 3, page 143); repeat from ★ around: 90 sts.

Rnd 2: K 14, P2, ★ K 16, P2; repeat from ★ around to last 2 sts, K2.

Rnd 3: ★ K 12, SSK, K2, K2 tog; repeat from ★ around: 80 sts.

Rnd 4: K 13, P2 tog (Fig. 6, page 143), ★ K 14, P2 tog; repeat from ★ around to last st, K1; remove marker: 75 sts.

Rnd 5: K6, place marker, K6, [slip 2 together as if to **knit**, K1, P2SSO (Figs. 5a & 5b, page 143)], ★ K 12, slip 2 together as if to **knit**, K1, P2SSO; repeat from ★ around to last 6 sts, K6: 65 sts.

Rnd 6: Knit around.

Rnd 7: K5, slip 2 together as if to **knit**, K1, P2SSO, ★ K 10, slip 2 together as if to **knit**, K1, P2SSO; repeat from ★ around to last 5 sts, K5: 55 sts.

Rnd 8: Knit around.

Rnd 9: K4, slip 2 together as if to **knit**, K1, P2SSO, ★ K8, slip 2 together as if to **knit**, K1, P2SSO; repeat from ★ around to last 4 sts, K4: 45 sts.

Rnd 10: Knit around.

Rnd 11: K3, slip 2 together as if to **knit**, K1, P2SSO, ★ K6, slip 2 together as if to **knit**, K1, P2SSO; repeat from ★ around to last 3 sts, K3: 35 sts.

Rnd 12: Knit around.

Rnd 13: K2, slip 2 together as if to **knit**, K1, P2SSO, ★ K4, slip 2 together as if to **knit**, K1, P2SSO; repeat from ★ around to last 2 sts, K2: 25 sts.

Rnd 14: Knit around.

Rnd 15: K1, slip 2 together as if to **knit**, K1, P2SSO, ★ K2, slip 2 together as if to **knit**, K1, P2SSO; repeat from ★ around to last st, K1: 15 sts.

Rnd 16: Knit around.

Rnd 17: ★ Slip 2 together as if to **knit**, K1, P2SSO; repeat from ★ around: 5 sts.

Cut yarn leaving a long end for sewing. Thread yarn needle with end and weave through remaining sts, gathering tightly to close; secure end.

Mittens
Right Mitten
CUFF
Cast 40 sts onto one double pointed needle.

Slip 13 sts onto each of two double pointed needles leaving remaining 14 sts on third needle.

Hold the needles, forming a triangle, with the working yarn coming from the stitch on the last needle and being careful not to twist the stitches around the needles.

Place a split ring marker around the first stitch to mark the beginning of the round (see Markers, page 143).

Rnd 1: ★ P2, K2, (P1, K2) twice; repeat from ★ once **more**, (P2, K2) around.

Repeat Rnd 1 until Mitten measures approximately 3" (7.5 cm) from cast on edge.

BODY
Rnd 1: P2, K2, P1, K 12, P1, K2, P2, knit around.

Rnd 2: K5, C6B, C6F, knit around.

Rnd 3: P2, K2, P1, K 12, P1, K2, P2, knit around.

Rnd 4: Knit around.

Rnd 5: P2, K2, P1, K 12, P1, K2, P2, place marker, increase in each of next 2 sts (Thumb Gusset) (Figs. 1a & 1b, page 143), place marker, knit around: 42 sts.

Rnd 6: Knit around.

Rnd 7: P2, K2, P1, K 12, P1, K2, P2, increase, K2, increase, knit around: 44 sts.

Rnd 8: K5, C6B, C6F, knit around.

Rnd 9: P2, K2, P1, K 12, P1, K2, P2, increase, K4, increase, knit around: 46 sts.

Rnd 10: Knit around.

Rnd 11: P2, K2, P1, K 12, P1, K2, P2, increase, K6, increase, knit around: 48 sts.

Rnd 12: Knit around.

Rnd 13: Work around to first marker, slip 22 sts just worked onto st holder, remove marker, K 10, remove marker, slip remaining 16 sts onto second st holder: 10 sts.

THUMB
Rnd 1: Turn; add on 2 sts (Figs. 2a & 2b, page 143), **turn**; knit around evenly distributing sts on three double pointed needles, place marker: 12 sts.

Knit around until Thumb measures approximately 2 1/2" (6.5 cm).

Decrease Rnd: K2 tog around: 6 sts.

Cut yarn leaving a long end for sewing. Thread yarn needle with end and weave through remaining sts, gathering tightly to close; secure end.

(continued on page 124)

Hand
Rnd 1: Evenly distributing sts on three double pointed needles, slip 22 sts from first st holder onto double pointed needles, pick up 2 sts at base of Thumb (Fig. 7, page 144), K 16 from second st holder: 40 sts.

Work even until Mitten measures approximately 9½" (24 cm) from cast on edge.

Top Shaping
Rnd 1: (K2, K2 tog) around: 30 sts.

Rnd 2: Knit around.

Rnd 3: (K1, K2 tog) around: 20 sts.

Rnd 4: Knit around.

Rnd 5: K2 tog around: 10 sts.

Rnd 6: Knit around.

Rnd 7: K2 tog around: 5 sts.

Cut yarn leaving a long end for sewing. Thread yarn needle with end and weave through remaining sts, gathering tightly to close; secure end.

Left Mitten
Cuff
Cast 40 sts onto one double pointed needle.

Slip 13 sts onto each of two double pointed needles leaving remaining 14 sts on third needle.

Place a split ring marker to mark the beginning of the round.

Rnd 1: K2, (P2, K2) 5 times, (P1, K2) twice, P2, (K2, P1) twice, K2, P2.

Repeat Rnd 1 until Mitten measures approximately 3" (7.5 cm) from cast on edge.

Body
Rnd 1: K 18, P2, K2, P1, K 12, P1, K2, P2.

Rnd 2: K 23, C6B, C6F, K5.

Rnd 3: K 18, P2, K2, P1, K 12, P1, K2, P2.

Rnd 4: Knit around.

Rnd 5: K 16, place marker, increase in each of next 2 sts (Thumb Gusset), place marker, P2, K2, P1, K 12, P1, K2, P2: 42 sts.

Rnd 6: Knit around.

Rnd 7: Knit to first marker, increase, K2, increase, P2, K2, P1, K 12, P1, K2, P2: 44 sts.

Rnd 8: K 27, C6B, C6F, K5.

Rnd 9: Knit to first marker, increase, K4, increase, P2, K2, P1, K 12, P1, K2, P2: 46 sts.

Rnd 10: Knit around.

Rnd 11: Knit to first marker, increase, K6, increase, work around: 48 sts.

Rnd 12: Knit around.

Rnd 13: Knit around to first marker, slip 16 sts just worked onto st holder, remove marker, K 10, remove marker, slip remaining 22 sts onto second st holder: 10 sts.

Thumb
Rnd 1: Turn; add on 2 sts, **turn;** knit around evenly distributing sts on three double pointed needles, place marker: 12 sts.

Knit around until Thumb measures approximately 2½" (6.5 cm).

Decrease Rnd: K2 tog around: 6 sts.

Cut yarn leaving a long end for sewing. Thread yarn needle with end and weave through remaining sts, gathering tightly to close; secure end.

HAND

Rnd 1: Evenly distributing sts on three double pointed needles, slip 16 sts from first st holder onto double pointed needles, pick up 2 sts at base of Thumb, work across 22 sts from second st holder: 40 sts.

Work even until Mitten measures approximately 9$^1/_2$" (24 cm) from cast on edge.

TOP SHAPING

Rnd 1: (K2, K2 tog) around: 30 sts.

Rnd 2: Knit around.

Rnd 3: (K1, K2 tog) around: 20 sts.

Rnd 4: Knit around.

Rnd 5: K2 tog around: 10 sts.

Rnd 6: Knit around.

Rnd 7: K2 tog around: 5 sts.

Cut yarn leaving a long end for sewing. Thread yarn needle with end and weave through remaining sts, gathering tightly to close; secure end.

Wreaths
(also shown on page 17)

Tuck sprigs of holly and fresh greenery into the branches of undecorated 12$^1/_2$" diameter wreaths. Tie a *Bell Ornament* and a big red ribbon bow to the top of each wreath, leaving long streamers.

Bell Ornaments
(also shown on page 17)

For each ornament, paint a foam bell with red acrylic paint. Add "snow" to the top with white acrylic paint. Brush glue over the snow and cover with mica flakes. Use a skewer to make a hole, from top to bottom, through the center of the ornament. Thread a jingle bell onto the center of a silver cord length. Thread both cord ends through the ornament and knot together, making a hanger at the top.

Chenille Candy Canes
(also shown on page 18)

- oversized red and green chenille stems (30mm)
- white decorative yarn
- fabric glue
- upholstery thread
- 1" dia. black pom-poms
- 1$^1/_8$" dia. black buttons
- 1" and 1$^1/_2$" dia. white pom-poms
- 6mm white chenille stems
- $^1/_4$" dia. wooden beads
- black and orange ball head pins
- wire cutters
- felt scraps

For each candy cane, bend a 30mm stem into a cane; then, wrap and glue yarn around it. To make the snowman, sew through a black pom-pom for the hat, a button hat brim, and 1 small and 2 large white pom-poms for the head and body. Run the thread back through all the pieces; then, knot and trim the ends. Trim the black pom-pom to shape the hat. Twist a 5" white stem length around the snowman's neck for the arms; glue a bead to each end. Trimming as needed and dotting glue on the ends, add the eyes and nose with the pins. Wrap a $^1/_2$"x5$^1/_4$" fringed felt scarf around the neck. Bend the snowman's arm around the candy cane.

Tree Skirt

(continued from page 19)

4. Aligning the side openings, center the red circle on the skirt. Sew the circle to the skirt along the side and center openings of the red circle. To hold the red circle in place, sew from the center opening to the outer edge of the red circle opposite the side opening.

5. Refer to the photos and transfer the enlarged reindeer, swirl and word patterns around the skirt. Needle Felt yarn along the pattern lines and apply fray preventative to the ends.

6. Draw six 3" diameter circles on cream felt. Needle Felt swirled red yarn inside the circles. Cut out the circles and cover the buttons with them. Sew 3 buttons to the skirt along the side opening. Cut buttonholes along the side opening across from the buttons. Sew the remaining buttons along the stitched line opposite the side opening.

Yo-Yo Trees

(also shown on page 21)
• tracing paper
• assorted print fabric scraps
• 32-gauge wire
• wire cutters
• hot glue gun
• 1/2" dia. buttons

126

• red and brown acrylic paint
• paintbrushes
• 1 1/2" wooden cubes
• clear dimensional glaze

1. Enlarge the patterns on page 149 to 200%. For each tree, use the patterns and cut 2 fabric circles of each size. Make Yo-Yos (page 141) from the circles.

2. Thread both ends of a 15" wire length, 1/4" apart, through the center of the largest Yo-Yo (gathered side up). Thread the remaining Yo-Yos from largest to smallest onto both wire ends. Twist the wire ends together and trim. Glue a button to the top of the tree.

3. Paint the cube red, lightly brush with brown and apply glaze. Glue the tree to the cube.

Felt Triangle Tree

(also shown on page 21)
• green felt
• polyester fiberfill
• cream embroidery floss
• 1/4" dia. wooden bead
• clear glass E bead
• red custard cup
• hot glue gun

Enlarge the pattern on page 149 to 200%. Use the pattern and cut 4 felt tree sides. Cut a 5" square felt base. Leaving an opening in the bottom, sew the

tree pieces together with a 1/4" seam allowance. Turn and stuff the tree and sew the opening closed. Use 6 strands of floss to stitch along the side seams as shown. Sew the beads to the top of the tree. Turn the cup upside down and glue the tree to the bottom.

Cone Trees

(also shown on page 21)

SWEATER TREE
• spoon or melon baller
• 4" dia.x15"h foam cone
• sweater
• shank and other assorted buttons
• ball head pins
• hot glue gun
• bead garland

Make a 1 3/4" dia.x1 1/2" deep hole in the center bottom of the cone. Cut a sleeve from the sweater. Cut the sleeve open along the seam and trim the sleeve to fit around the cone, adding a 1/4" seam allowance and 3 1/2" at the bottom. Avoiding the seam allowance and 4" at the bottom, sew buttons to the sweater piece. Matching right sides, sew the side edges of the sleeve together; turn right side out and place on the cone. Wrap the bottom sleeve edge to the bottom of the cone; tuck and pin the edge in the hole.

Sew a shank button at the top of the cone. Gluing the ends at the top and bottom, wrap and pin the garland around the cone.

SCALLOPED TREE
- straight pins
- light and dark green felt
- 4" dia.x12"h foam cone
- tracing paper
- pinking shears
- red embroidery floss
- 3/4" dia. red felt beads
- red and green ball head pins
- 1/4" dia. green wooden beads

Wrap and pin a 3" wide light green felt strip around the bottom of the cone. Repeating the pattern as needed, use the pattern on page 149 and the pinking shears and cut scalloped felt strips to fit around the cone (be sure to alternate colors). Use 6 strands of floss to add *Running Stitches* (page 142) along the dark green scallops. Wrap the strips around the cone and pin at the back. For the top strip, sew *Running Stitches* along the top straight edge. Pull the stitches to gather tightly so the strip fits over the top of the cone; knot and trim the ends. Turn right side out. Hold the gathered strip and a felt bead in place on top of the cone with a ball head pin. Use ball head pins to add beads to the tree as you'd like.

Barn Wreath
(also shown on page 23)

Use floral wire to cover an 18" diameter metal wreath form with greenery. Accent the greenery with pine needles, berries and pinecones.

Welcome Sign
(also shown on page 30)
- 3/8 yd red fabric
- tracing paper
- white wax-free transfer paper
- cream embroidery floss
- paper-backed fusible web
- pinking shears
- 1/4 yd red and white print fabric
- acid-free spray adhesive
- foam core board cut to fit in frame
- frame with a 7 1/2"x9 1/2" front opening
- 3/8"w green polka-dot ribbon
- 1 1/4" tall bell ornament
- ball head pin
- 1 1/2"w reversible red and white polka-dot ribbon
- staple gun

1. Cut an 8"x10" and an 11 1/2"x13 1/2" piece from red fabric. Transfer the pattern on page 150 onto the center of the small piece. *Stem Stitch* (page 142) along the transferred lines with 2 strands of floss.

2. Fuse web to the back of the stitched piece. Use the pinking shears to trim the fabric to 5 3/8"x8".

3. Fuse the stitched piece to the center front of a 7 3/8"x10" print fabric piece; fuse web to the back. Use the pinking shears to trim the print fabric 1/4" outside the edges of the stitched piece. Fuse the print fabric to the center of the large red fabric piece.

4. Using spray adhesive in a well-ventilated area, cover the foam core with the fabric. Insert the foam core in the frame. Knot 3/8" ribbon through the ornament hanger and pin the ornament to the framed piece.

5. For the hanger, leaving 2" tails at the back, staple the ends of a 16" length of 1 1/2" ribbon to the back of the frame.

Embroidered Framed Piece
(also shown on page 32)
- white wax-free transfer paper
- 8 1/2"x11 1/2" red fabric piece
- cream and red embroidery floss
- paper-backed fusible web
- pinking shears
- light box or a sunny window and removable tape
- 11 1/2"x13 1/2" cream fabric piece

(continued on page 128)

- water-soluble fabric marking pen
- ⁵/₈", 1" and 1¹/₄" dia. self-covered buttons
- red and cream print fabric scraps
- wire cutters
- hot glue gun
- acid-free spray adhesive
- foam core board cut to fit in frame
- frame with a 7¹/₂"x9¹/₂" front opening

1. Enlarge the pattern on page 151 to 166%. Using transfer paper, transfer the saying only onto the center of the red fabric. *Stem Stitch (page 142)* the saying with 3 strands and the name with 1 strand of cream floss. Fuse web to the back of the fabric. Use the pinking shears to trim the fabric to 4⁵/₈"x7³/₈".
2. Use the light box or tape the pattern and fabric to the window to transfer the swirls and dots onto the center of the cream fabric with the pen. Use 3 strands of red floss to embroider the design with *Stem Stitch* and *French Knots*.
3. Fuse the red fabric to the center of the cream fabric.
4. Cover the buttons with fabric scraps. Remove the shanks and hot glue the buttons over the ends of the swirls as shown.

5. Using spray adhesive in a well-ventilated area, cover the foam core with the cream fabric. Insert the foam core in the frame.

Scrap Quilt
(also shown on page 34)
- ¹/₂ yd each of nine 44"/45"w fabrics
- rotary cutter, ruler and cutting mat or scissors
- 4¹/₄ yds of 44"/45"w backing fabric
- cotton batting
- yarn
- sharp yarn needle
- 7¹/₂ yds of extra-wide double-fold bias binding

Match right sides and use a ¹/₂" seam allowance. Wash and press all fabrics before beginning. The finished size of our quilt is 58"x72".

1. For the quilt top, matching the selvage edges, fold each of the ¹/₂-yard pieces in half and cut along the fold; then, cut off the selvages. Cut each piece from edge to edge into strips about 20" long with different widths…they shouldn't be perfect rectangles, so cut each strip a little narrower on one end, but at least 1" wide (Fig. 1).

Fig. 1

2. Match long edges and sew random strips together to make 3 striped sections at least 72" long. Trim, then match the long edges and sew the striped sections together.
3. To back the quilt, cut the backing into two 2¹/₈-yard pieces. Trim the selvages. Sew the pieces together along the long edges to make a tube (Fig. 2a). Follow Fig. 2b to match the seams and press; cut along the fold on one side. Open up the pieced backing (Fig. 2c).

Fig. 2a   **Fig 2b**

Fig. 2c

4. With the backing wrong side up, center and layer the batting and quilt top (right side up) on the backing; pin the layers together. Use yarn lengths to join the quilt and backing as desired and tie them off. Baste the layers together close to the edges of the quilt top. Trim the batting and backing to the same size as the quilt top.
5. Sandwich the quilt edges in the fold of the binding and zigzag the binding to the quilt, slightly rounding the corners.

Holly Pillow
(also shown on page 35)
• 1/2 yd red and white print fabric
• 12"x16" pillow form
• 2/3 yd white fabric
• tracing paper
• red corduroy scraps
• light box or a sunny window and removable tape
• water-soluble fabric marking pen
• clear nylon thread
• white and red embroidery floss
• 1 3/8 yds of 1 1/2"w white grosgrain ribbon
• liquid fray preventative

Match right sides and use a 1/2" seam allowance.

1. Leaving one end open, sew two 13"x17" print fabric pieces together. Turn right side out, insert the pillow form and sew the opening closed.
2. For the pillow cover front and lining, cut two 14 1/2"x22 1/2" white fabric pieces.
3. Enlarge the pattern on page 150 to 264%. Use one whole leaf pattern and cut 3 corduroy leaves. Use the light box or tape the entire pattern and fabric to the window to transfer the pattern 3" from the bottom short edge at the center of the cover front.
4. Zigzag the holly leaves in place on the cover front with clear thread and sew *Running Stitches* (page 142) along the edges with 3 strands of white floss. Use 3 strands of red floss to embroider the swirls and dots with *Stem Stitch* and *French Knots*.

5. Cut four 12" ribbon lengths for the ties. Mark the tie placement on the long edges of the cover front, 5" from each short edge. Matching the ribbon end to the raw fabric edge, pin a tie at each mark. Sew the cover front and lining together along the long edges. Turn right side out.
6. Matching the short edges of the cover front, fold the cover in half. Leaving the lining open, sew the short edges of the cover front together between the side seams. Turn the raw edges of the lining under, hand sew the opening closed and turn the cover right side out. Insert the pillow in the cover and knot the ties. Apply fray preventative to the tie ends.

Memorabilia Tablescape
(also shown on pages 38-39)
Create a centerpiece that is sure to bring about fond memories. Cover the backing from an extra-long frame (ours is 13 3/4"x38") with a vintage Christmas tablecloth or fabric and insert it in the frame. Round up trinkets and treasures from Christmases past and arrange them on the covered frame backing.

Felt Stockings
(also shown on page 43)
- felt (¹/₄ yd for each stocking)
- felt scraps
- tracing paper
- fabric glue
- dimensional glittery fabric paint
- sequins
- jingle bells
- ball fringe

For each stocking, enlarge the stocking pattern on page 152 to 252%. Use the pattern and cut 2 felt stockings. Matching edges, sew the stockings together and add a felt hanger. Decorate the stockings with shapes cut from felt (use the snowman or the enlarged tree pattern or create your own designs) and add paint, sequins, bells and ball fringe.

Evergreen Spray
(also shown on page 45)
Offer friends and family a fragrant welcome with a fresh greenery door spray. Wire together evergreen sprigs (we used pine, cedar and rosemary) and add a looped wire hanger. Press dried whole cloves into fresh limes and clementines; then, wire them to the spray. Knot extra-wide ribbon at the top of the spray.

Grownup Apron
(also shown on page 47)
- tracing paper
- ⁵/₈ yd each of 2 print fabrics for apron and lining
- 1⁵/₈ yds of ¹/₂"w single-fold bias tape
- ⁵/₈ yd of ¹/₄"w and 1⁷/₈ yds of ¹/₂"w double-fold bias tape
- 2 yds of 1¹/₂"w twill tape
- embroidery floss
- two 1³/₈"x1³/₄" oval buttons
- liquid fray preventative

1. Enlarge the half pattern on page 153 to 296%. Read Making Patterns on page 141 and make a whole apron pattern. Use the pattern and cut a fabric apron and lining piece.
2. Zigzag single-fold bias tape to the apron piece along the vertical, then horizontal gray lines shown on the pattern.
3. Use the pattern and cut a pocket from the apron fabric. Sew ¹/₄" double-fold bias tape over the sides, bottom, then top edge of the pocket. Sew the pocket to the apron.
4. Matching right sides and using a ¹/₄" seam allowance, sew the apron and lining pieces together along the top edges only. Turn right side out and press. Pin the raw edges together and sew ¹/₂" double-fold bias tape over the edges.

5. For the ties, cut the twill tape in half. Fold one end of each tie ¹/₂", then 2" to the back. Sew the folded end of one tie to each corner at the top of the apron front. Use floss to sew a button to each folded end. Trim the loose ends and apply fray preventative.

Ripple Crocheted Throw
(also shown on page 52)
Read Crochet on pages 144-145 before beginning.
Finished Size: 48"x60" (122 cm x 152.5 cm)

⬛⬛◻◻ **EASY**

Materials

Bulky Weight Yarn
[3¹/₂ ounces, 148 yards (100 grams, 135 meters) per skein]:
    Lt Teal - 2 skeins
    Dk Teal - 2 skeins
    Lt Taupe - 2 skeins
    Dk Taupe - 2 skeins
    Lt Blue - 2 skeins
    Dk Blue - 2 skeins
    Lt Green - 2 skeins
    Dk Green - 2 skeins
Crochet hook, size K (6.5 mm) **or** size needed for gauge
Yarn needle

Gauge: 33 sts (3 repeats) = 8" (20.25 cm); 12 rows = 5¹/₄" (13.25 cm)

Gauge Swatch: *8"x5¼"*
   (20.25 cm x 13.25 cm)
   Ch 32.
Rows 1-12: Work same as Throw.

Finish off.

Color Sequence
★ Work 3 rows of each of the
following: Lt Teal, Dk Teal,
Lt Taupe, Dk Taupe, Lt Blue,
Dk Blue, Lt Green, Dk Green;
repeat from ★ for Color Sequence.

Throw
With Lt Teal, ch 197 **loosely**.

Row 1 (Right side): Sc in second ch
from hook and in next 3 chs, 3 sc
in next ch, sc in next 4 chs, ★ skip
next 2 chs, sc in next 4 chs, 3 sc
in next ch, sc in next 4 chs; repeat
from ★ across: 198 sc.

Note: Loop a short piece of yarn
around any stitch to mark Row 1
as **right** side.

Rows 2 and 3: Ch 1, turn; skip first
sc, working in Back Loops Only
(Fig. 4, page 145), sc in next 4 sc,
3 sc in next sc, ★ sc in next 4 sc,
skip next 2 sc, sc in next 4 sc, 3 sc
in next sc; repeat from ★ across
to last 5 sc, sc in next 3 sc, skip
next sc, sc in **both** loops of last sc.

Finish off.

Row 4: With **wrong** side facing, join
next color with slip st in **both** loops
of first sc; ch 1, working in Back
Loops Only, sc in next 4 sc, 3 sc
in next sc, ★ sc in next 4 sc, skip
next 2 sc, sc in next 4 sc, 3 sc in
next sc; repeat from ★ across to
last 5 sc, sc in next 3 sc, skip next
sc, sc in **both** loops of last sc.

Rows 5 and 6: Ch 1, turn; skip first
sc, working in Back Loops Only, sc
in next 4 sc, 3 sc in next sc, ★ sc
in next 4 sc, skip next 2 sc, sc in
next 4 sc, 3 sc in next sc; repeat
from ★ across to last 5 sc, sc in
next 3 sc, skip next sc, sc in **both**
loops of last sc.

Finish off.

Row 7: With **right** side facing, join
next color with slip st in **both** loops
of first sc; ch 1, working in Back
Loops Only, sc in next 4 sc, 3 sc
in next sc, ★ sc in next 4 sc, skip
next 2 sc, sc in next 4 sc, 3 sc in
next sc; repeat from ★ across to
last 5 sc, sc in next 3 sc, skip next
sc, sc in **both** loops of last sc.

Repeat Rows 2-7 for pattern until
Throw measures approximately
60" (152.5 cm) from beginning ch,
ending by working Row 3 or Row 6.

Finish off.

Muff
(also shown on page 54)
• sweater
• ½ yd chenille fabric
• cotton batting
• tissue paper
• two 5" fabric squares
• pinking shears
• felt and fabric scraps
• 1½" dia. self-covered button

Use a ½" seam allowance.

1. For the muff, cut a 14"x20"
sweater piece, a 16"x20"
chenille piece and two 16"x20"
batting pieces.
2. With the batting on the wrong
side of the chenille, match right
sides and sew the long edges of the
batting, chenille and sweater pieces
together. Turn right side out.
3. Matching raw edges, fold the
muff in half, forming a tube with
the sweater on the inside. Leaving
the chenille open, sew the raw
edges of the sweater together
between the side seams. Turn the
raw chenille edges under, hand sew
the opening closed and turn so the
sweater is on the outside of the
muff. Fold the ends of the muff to
the outside.

(continued on page 132)

131

4. For the flower, trace the pattern on page 155 onto tissue paper. Stack the fabric squares, wrong sides together, and pin the tissue paper pattern to the fabric. Sew along the traced lines through the paper and the fabric. Tear away the tissue paper and use the pinking shears to cut out the flower outside the stitched lines.

5. Use the pinking shears to cut a 1³/₄" diameter felt circle. Cover the button with the fabric scrap. Sew the felt and button to the center of the flower and tack the flower to one end of the muff.

Flip-Flop Doll

(also shown on page 56)
- ¹/₄ yd fabric for the doll
- ¹/₄ yd each of 2 print fabrics for the shirts
- two ⁵/₁₆" dia. buttons for eyes
- red, black and pink embroidery floss
- pink colored pencil
- polyester fiberfill
- fabric glue
- ¹/₈"w rickrack
- four ¹/₄" dia. buttons
- yarn
- 10" cardboard square
- ¹/₈"w and ³/₈"w ribbon
- fabric scraps

- ³/₈ yd each of 2 print fabrics for the skirts
- 30" length of 2"w ruffled trim
- embroidered flowers (ours were cut from a floral trim)

Fold this doll's skirt to one end and she's awake; fold it to the other end and she's asleep. Match right sides and use a ¹/₈" seam allowance unless otherwise indicated.

1. Enlarge the patterns on page 154 to 241%. Use the patterns and cut 2 doll pieces from the doll fabric and 2 shirts from each shirt fabric.

2. For the awake doll, sew the button eyes to one head on one doll piece. Embroider the mouth with *Satin* and *Straight Stitches* (page 142) and add *Straight Stitch* eyelashes. Blush the cheeks with the pencil.

3. Add features to the sleeping doll, omitting the buttons and adding *Stem Stitch* eyelids.

4. Leaving an opening for turning, sew the doll pieces together. Clip corners and curves and turn right side out. Stuff the doll and sew the opening closed.

5. Sew the shirts together in pairs along the shoulder and side edges. Sew a ¹/₄" hem at the bottom of each shirt. Clip corners and turn right side out.

6. At the neck, cut a 1¹/₂"-long slit down the center back of each shirt; then, put the shirts on the dolls. Fold the neck of each shirt ¹/₈" to the wrong side. Glue rickrack along the sleeve, neck and slit edges. Pull the slit closed at the neck and sew a ¹/₄" button at the top. Sew 2 buttons to the front of the sleeping doll's shirt.

7. For each doll's hair, wrap yarn around the cardboard square 10 times. Slide the yarn off the cardboard. Sew across the center and cut the loops. Glue separate yarn lengths to the top of the head/face for bangs; then, glue the sewn yarn to the back of the head. Tie narrow ribbon or fabric strips around the hair to make pigtails. Trim the hair as needed.

8. Cut a 9"x29" piece from each skirt fabric. Matching short edges, sew each skirt piece into a tube. For each waist, turn one tube edge ¹/₂" to the wrong side and topstitch. Turn each skirt piece right side out.

9. Press the bottom edges of the skirt pieces ¹/₂" to the wrong side. Fold and glue the trim ends ³/₈" to the wrong side twice. Matching wrong sides and sandwiching the trim between the skirts, sew the bottom edges together.

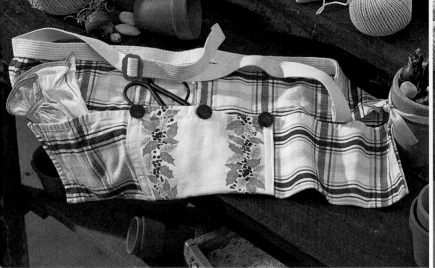

10. Sew a Running Stitch around the top of each skirt; don't cut the thread ends. Slide the skirt onto the doll. Separate and arrange the skirt tops so the top of each doll's skirt is at her waist. Pull the threads to gather each skirt around the waist; then, knot and trim the threads. Tie ³/₈"w ribbon into a bow over the stitches around each waist.

11. Add embroidered flowers to the doll as desired.

Gardener's Gift Set
(also shown on page 58)
- 16¹/₂"x24" reversible woven tea towel for the apron
- woven tea towel for the pocket
- three ⁷/₈" dia. buttons
- 58" length of 1"w canvas trim
- slide-on buckle
- cardstock
- craft glue
- scrapbook papers
- 3-section wooden box with handles
- 2 decorative brads
- wire cutters
- wood excelsior
- fine-point permanent pen
- die-cut tags
- jute twine
- river rocks
- flower bulbs

- rickrack
- twill tape
- clay pot to fit in box

1. Wash, then press the towels.
2. For the outer center pocket, cut a 9" square from the pocket towel. Press one edge ¹/₂" to the wrong side twice; topstitch. Press the raw edges ¹/₂" to the wrong side. With both pieces right side up, center the hemmed edge of the pocket on one long edge of the apron towel. Topstitch along the side and bottom edges of the pocket.
3. Fold the apron lengthwise as shown, so the top of the pocket is 5" below the top of the apron. Sew the apron sides together. Sew through all layers along the side edges of the outer center pocket to divide the folded area into 3 pockets. Sew a button through all layers at each top corner of the outer center pocket. Sew a button at the middle of the outer center pocket through the pockets only.
4. For the tie, thread one end of the trim through the buckle. Fold the end ¹/₂", then 1¹/₄" to the back and topstitch. Fold the remaining end ¹/₂" to the back twice and topstitch. Center and pin the trim along the top edge of the apron; sew in place.
5. Sizing as needed, photocopy the saying on page 156 onto

cardstock and cut it out. Glue the saying to layered scrapbook paper pieces and glue to the box front. Remove the brad prongs and glue a brad to each end of the layered piece.
6. Place excelsior in the box sections. Write messages on the tags. Knot twine through the hole in one of the tags; place the rocks, bulbs and tag in the center section of the box. Adding tags, tie rickrack around the apron and twill tape around the pot and place them in the end sections.

Felted Granny Square Tote
(continued from page 59)

Square (Make 35)
With smaller size hook and Blue, ch 4; join with slip st to form a ring.

Rnd 1 (Right side): Ch 3 **(counts as first dc, now and throughout)**, 2 dc in ring, ch 3, (3 dc in ring, ch 3) 3 times; join with slip st to first dc, finish off: 4 ch-3 sps.

Note: Loop a short piece of yarn around any stitch to mark Rnd 1 as **right** side.

(continued on page 134)

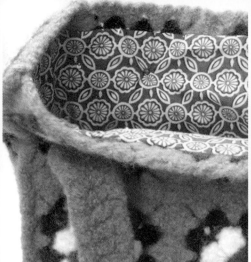

Rnd 2: With **right** side facing, join Cream with slip st in any corner ch-3 sp; ch 3, (2 dc, ch 3, 3 dc) in same sp, (3 dc, ch 3, 3 dc) in each of next 3 ch-3 sps; join with slip st to first dc, finish off.

Rnd 3: With **right** side facing, join Rose with slip st in any corner ch-3 sp; ch 3, (2 dc, ch 3, 3 dc) in same sp, skip next 3 dc, 3 dc in sp **before** next dc (Fig. 5, page 145), ★ (3 dc, ch 3, 3 dc) in next ch-3 sp, skip next 3 dc, 3 dc in sp **before** next dc; repeat from ★ 2 times **more**; join with slip st to first dc, finish off.

Rnd 4: With **right** side facing, join Green with slip st in any corner ch-3 sp; ch 3, (2 dc, ch 3, 3 dc) in same sp, ch 1, (skip next 3 dc, 3 dc in sp **before** next dc, ch 1) twice, ★ (3 dc, ch 3, 3 dc) in next ch-3 sp, ch 1, (skip next 3 dc, 3 dc in sp **before** next dc, ch 1) twice; repeat from ★ 2 times **more**; join with slip st to first dc, finish off.

Assembly

With Green and working through **both** loops, whipstitch Squares together **very loosely** (Fig. 7, page 145) forming 8 vertical strips of 4 Squares each and one strip of 3 Squares (Bottom), beginning

134

in center ch of one corner sp and ending in center ch of next corner sp; then whipstitch 3 strips together to form Front of Tote and 3 strips together to form Back of Tote; leave remaining 2 strips (Gussets) and Bottom unattached (Fig. 1).

Fig. 1

Front

Gussets

Back

Bottom

Match **wrong** sides of Front and one Gusset together. Using larger size hook and working through **both** pieces, join a double strand of Green with sc in corner ch-3 sp (see Joining With Sc, page 145); sc in each sc and in each sp and joining across to next corner sp, sc in corner sp; finish off.

Join Gusset to Back in same manner, then join second Gusset to opposite side of Front and Back to form Tote.

Match **wrong** sides of Tote and Bottom together. Using larger size hook and working through both pieces, join a double strand of Green with sc in corner ch-3 sp; sc in each sc and in each sp and joining around; join with slip st to first sc, finish off.

Strap (Make 2)
With larger size hook and a double strand of Green, ch 72.

Row 1: Dc in fourth ch from hook and in each ch across: 70 sts.

Edging: Ch 1, working **around** st just made, (slip st, ch 1) 3 times; working in free loops of beginning ch (Fig. 6, page 145), (slip st in next ch, ch 1) across; (slip st, ch 1) 3 times around first st; working across Row 1, (slip st in next dc, ch 1) across; join with slip st to first slip st, finish off.

Felting

Setting your top loading washing machine for the lowest water level, follow *Felting* on page 141 to felt the pieces. Once the Tote is felted, a box (or any other item of the correct size) can be covered with plastic and inserted into the Tote to help shape it. Lay the Straps out flat to dry.

Lining

Cut fabric 15"wx32½"l (38 cm x 82.5 cm) or size to fit. Matching right sides and short edges, fold fabric in half. Sew side seams using ½" (12 mm) seam allowance. For squared bottom, match side seam to center bottom forming a point at base of the lining (Fig. 2). Sew across, 1¾" (4.5 cm) down from the tip of the point. Repeat on other side. Fold points against bottom and insert lining into Tote. Roll down top edge of fabric to top edge of Tote and pin. Sew the lining to the felted Tote using sewing thread.

Fig. 2

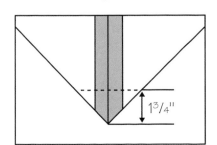

1¾"

Cover a 3½"x10½" (9 cm x 26.5 cm) cardboard piece with fabric, gluing to secure. Place in the bottom of the Tote.

Working through Buttons, sew Straps to Tote, using photo as a guide for placement.

Tag Wreath
(also shown on page 61)

For a one-of-a-kind holiday display, gather your scrapbooking supplies and make a wreath-ful of crafty tags. (We used tag dies and a die-cutting tool and backed our paper tags with cardstock to make them sturdier.) Overlapping and filling in as needed, tie the tags onto a metal wreath form with ribbons. Add small tags to some of the larger tags with adhesive foam dots. For an extra-wide ribbon bow, we zigzagged two twill tape lengths together side by side.

Merry Christmas Card
(also shown on page 62)
• textured and plain cardstock
• scrapbook papers
• craft glue
• brown ink pad
• rub-on letters
• buttons
• 2½"-tall chipboard letters (JOY)
• fine-point permanent pen
• stapler and staples
• ribbons and rickrack

1. For the card, cut two 5½" textured cardstock squares and a 1"x5" scrapbook paper spine. Leaving ¼" between the squares, glue the spine to one edge of each square. Fold the card in half.
2. Ink the edges of trimmed scrapbook paper pieces and glue them to the inside and outside card front. Make a 2¼"x5½" scrapbook paper pocket and glue it to the inside card back.
3. Add a message to the card front with rub-ons. Ink the card and glue on buttons as desired.
4. For the tag, cut away the corners on one end of a 4¼"x5" plain cardstock piece. Decorate the tag with scrapbook paper, ink, chipboard letters, rub-ons and the pen. Staple ribbons and rickrack to the top of the tag and place the tag in the card pocket.

Photo Window Card
(also shown on page 64)
- craft glue
- deckle-edged scissors
- cardstock
- 4$\frac{1}{4}$"x5$\frac{1}{2}$" blank purchased card with envelope
- 1$\frac{3}{8}$" square punch
- rub-on message
- tracing paper
- holiday photo (enlarged or reduced to fit in card window)
- transfer paper (optional)
- fine-point permanent pen

Center and glue a 1$\frac{7}{8}$" deckle-edged cardstock square on the card front $\frac{7}{8}$" from the top edge. Punch a window in the card front at the center of the deckle-edged square. Apply the rub-on message below the window. Use the inner circle of the pattern on page 156 and cut a circle from the photo. Glue the photo to the inside card back so it shows through the window. Transfer or freehand the ornament design around the photo and add a message with the pen. Glue a deckle-edged cardstock strip to the envelope front and draw accent lines along the sides of the strip.

Holiday Memories Gift Bag
(also shown on page 65)

Remove the handles from a gift bag. Layer and glue scrapbook paper and an enlarged photocopy of a favorite holiday photo on the bag front. Zigzagging along the center to secure, cover a shipping tag with scrapbook paper strips, ribbon, rickrack and stickers. Sew buttons to the tag and tie rickrack around a button at the top. Attach the tag to the bag with a large, plastic-coated paperclip.

Childhood Gift Bag
(also shown on page 65)

Remove the handles from a gift bag; then, cover the bag front with scrapbook paper. Make a layered cardstock and scrapbook paper tag and adhere stickers to the tag. Paint a clothespin with acrylic paint; then, glue on scrapbook paper strips. Adhere a chipboard flower to the clothespin with an adhesive foam dot and clip the tag onto the bag.

Pom-Pom Package
(also shown on page 67)
- spray adhesive
- papier-mâché box
- scrapbook papers
- yarn
- 1"h and 2"h cardboard strips

1. Using spray adhesive in a well-ventilated area, cover the box with scrapbook papers.
2. For the large pom-pom, place a 6" piece of yarn along the top edge of the 2" cardboard strip. Wrap yarn around and around the strip and the yarn piece (Fig. 1) (the more you wrap, the fluffier the pom-pom). Tie the wound yarn together tightly with the 6" piece. Cut the loops opposite the tie; then, fluff and trim the pom-pom into shape. Repeat, using the 1" cardboard strip to make 2 small pom-poms.

Fig. 1

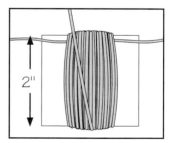

3. Wrap yarn around the box; then, knot and trim the ends. Thread the large pom-pom onto the center of a 26" yarn length. Thread a small pom-pom onto each end of the yarn 6" from the large pom-pom. Thread the yarn ends back through the large pom-pom and knot and trim the ends. Tie the pom-poms to the yarn on the box.

Pinwheel Package

(also shown on page 67)

Gluing the ends at the bottom, wrap scrapbook paper around a plain white box. Tie ribbon and fibers around the box. For the pinwheel, cut a $3^3/4$" square of double-sided scrapbook paper. Matching points, fold the square in half twice. Unfold the square and cut 2" along each fold line. Fold every other point to the center and attach a glittered brad through all the layers. Add a name with rub-ons to one end of a craft stick and adhere the pinwheel to the other end with an adhesive foam dot. Slide the stick under the ribbon and fibers on the package and secure with an adhesive foam dot.

Package Wraps

(also shown on pages 70-71)

For a fresh approach to holiday gift wrapping, place gifts inside custom-sized handmade package wraps.

- 2 coordinating fabric pieces or 1 reversible tea towel for each package
- fabric strips (optional)
- rickrack
- embroidery floss
- large buttons
- ribbons
- twill tape
- tissue paper
- fabric for flowers
- jingle bells (optional)

1. For each package made with fabric, match right sides and sew 2 fabric rectangles together, leaving an opening for turning. Turn right side out and sew the opening closed.
2. Fold the bottom edge of the fabric or towel up to form a pocket to fit your gift. Sew the sides of the pocket together. Fold the top down for a flap.
3. Adding fabric strips or rickrack as desired, use floss to sew buttons to the pocket. Sew ribbon, rickrack or twill tape button loops to the flap.
4. To add a flower, enlarge the pattern on page 156 to 200%; then, trace onto tissue paper. Stack two 10" fabric squares, wrong sides together, and pin the tissue paper pattern to the fabric. Sew along the traced lines through the paper and the fabric. Tear away the tissue paper and cut out the flower outside the stitched lines. Pinch the center of each petal to pleat and sew the pleat in place. Turn up one corner of the package flap and tack the flower, along with a button and bell if you'd like, to the turned corner.

Flavored Oil Set

(also shown on page 73)

- light and dark brown cardstock scraps
- craft glue
- fine-point permanent pen
- olive oil decanter filled with Rosemary-Flavored Oil (page 73)
- $3/8$"w and $3/4$"w ribbons
- removable double-stick tape
- jar of olives
- handmade paper
- string
- wooden bread dish (ours is 5"x12")
- wood excelsior
- 2 dipping dishes
- tacky wax
- packaged bread
- wooden plate large enough for the bread and bread dish to fit on (ours is $10^1/8$" square)
- pinking shears
- sealing wax
- rubber stamp or seal

1. Make a layered oval cardstock label for the oil decanter. Glue a narrow ribbon loop bow to the top and tape the label to the decanter.
2. Remove the olive jar label. Wrap a handmade paper circle over the jar lid and tie in place with string.

(continued on page 138)

3. Fill the bread dish with excelsior and arrange the decanter, olives and dipping dishes inside. Securing with tacky wax, place the bread dish at the front and the bread at the back of the plate.

4. For the tag, cut a 2" diameter circle from each cardstock color. Trim the light circle with the pinking shears and glue it to the dark circle. Follow the manufacturer's instructions to drip sealing wax on the center of the tag and press the stamp or seal into the wax.

5. Wrap 3/4" ribbon around the set and glue the ends to the back of the tag.

Peppermint Package
(also shown on page 74)
- red acrylic paint
- paintbrushes
- metal container with ball feet (ours is 4¹/4"x4¹/4"x3¹/2")
- decoupage glue
- tracing paper
- red and white cardstock scraps
- craft glue
- fine-point permanent pen
- cellophane bags
- 1/8"w red and white ribbon
- Chocolate-Peppermint Bark (page 74)
- twist tie

1. Paint the inside, rim and feet of the container. Allow to dry; then, seal the painted areas with decoupage glue.

2. For the tag, use the pattern on page 156 to make a cardstock peppermint. Write a message on the back. Cut a 4" square from a cellophane bag, wrap it around the peppermint and knot ribbon around the ends.

3. Fill a bag with Chocolate-Peppermint Bark and close with the twist tie. Tie ribbon around the bag, attaching the cardstock peppermint to one end. Place the bag in the container.

Pizzelle Cones
(also shown on page 74)
- 7/16"w ribbon
- Pizzelles rolled into cones (page 74)
- wired pom-pom trim
- pencil
- cardstock
- 1/8" dia. hole punch
- rub-on words
- embroidery floss
- milk chocolate drops

Thread the ends of a ribbon hanger through the holes in each Pizzelle cone; knot the ends. Curl a trim length around the pencil; then, wrap the trim around the hanger.

For the tag, round the short ends of a 3/4"x1³/8" cardstock piece and punch a hole in one end. Add a rub-on to the tag and tie it to the hanger with floss. Fill the cone with chocolate drops.

Toffee Box
(also shown on page 75)
- brown acrylic paint
- paintbrushes
- unfinished wooden stationery box with sliding lid (ours is 6³/4"x8⁵/8")
- alphabet stamps
- brown ink pad
- spray adhesive
- scrapbook paper
- sandpaper
- disposable foam brush
- decoupage glue
- cellophane bag filled with Easy Microwave Butter Toffee (page 75)
- 1/8"w and 3/8"w ribbons

Thin the paint with water and brush over the box. Stamp "TOFFEE" on the sides of the box. Using spray adhesive in a well-ventilated area, cover the lid with scrapbook paper. Lightly sand the paper edges. Brush decoupage glue over the paper. Place the toffee in the box. Close the lid and tie ribbons around the box.

Cheese Ball Plate

(also shown on page 78)

- White Chocolate Chip Cheese Ball (page 78)
- colorful plate (our flower-shaped polka-dot plate is 8¹/₈" dia.)
- cellophane
- twist tie
- ⁵/₈"w ribbon
- white and other colors of felt to match plate
- craft glue
- red cardstock
- rub-on holiday message
- 20-gauge wire
- wire cutters
- needle-nose pliers
- bead
- awl

1. Place the cheese ball on the plate, wrap with cellophane and close with the twist tie. Tie a ribbon bow around the cellophane.
2. For the tag, cut away the corners on one end of a white felt piece. Glue the tag to cardstock and cut the cardstock a little larger all around. Apply the rub-on to the tag and sew on different-sized felt circles.

3. Curl one end of a wire length and thread the bead onto the wire. Make a hole through the top of the tag with the awl. Thread the opposite wire end through the hole and bend the end around the ribbon bow.

Lunch Box

(also shown on page 79)

- tracing and transfer paper
- black metal lunchbox with removable tray (our box is 8¹/₂"lx6¹/₄"wx8¹/₄"h)
- silver paint pen
- packaged cheese, summer sausage and spicy mustard
- scrapbook papers
- ¹/₁₆"w silver ribbon
- Sesame-Parmesan Rounds (page 78)
- 5¹/₄"x13¹/₂" cellophane bag
- tape
- paper shreds
- snowflake ornament
- greenery sprigs

1. Transfer the pattern on page 156 onto the box lid. Paint the design and refer to the photos to freehand draw the borders on the lunch box with the pen.
2. Wrap the cheese, sausage and mustard with scrapbook papers and ribbon. Place a 5"x8¹/₄" scrapbook paper piece and Sesame-Parmesan Rounds in the bag. Fold and tape the top to the back.

3. Fill the box and tray with paper shreds. Arrange the Sesame-Parmesan Rounds, tray, cheese, sausage and mustard in the lunch box.
4. Tie the ornament and greenery sprigs to the handle with ribbon.

Cookie Tassel

(also shown on page 80)

- ¹/₂"w sheer polka-dot ribbon
- upholstery needle
- large wooden beads
- Laurie's Special Sugar Cookies (page 80)
- cellophane
- tape
- embroidery floss

1. For the tassel, fold a 36" ribbon length in half. Thread a bead onto both ribbon ends, 9¹/₂" from the fold. Thread each ribbon end through opposite sides of another bead and knot below the bead.
2. Thread the folded ribbon end through a stack of cookies (alternate round and star-shaped cookies). Wrap the cookies in cellophane; then, tape the side and tie the ends closed with floss. Knot the ribbon above the cookies and thread 2 beads onto the folded end.
3. Knot additional ribbon lengths to the bottom of the tassel as desired.

Jar Topper

(also shown on page 80)
- 6¼" dia. fabric circle
- half-pint canning jar filled with Homemade Strawberry Jam (page 80)
- fabric glue
- ⅞"w velvet ribbon
- three ½" dia. jingle bells
- embroidery floss
- ⅜"w velveteen ribbon

Press the edge of the fabric circle ¼" to the wrong side; topstitch. Wrap the circle over the top of the jar and glue ⅞" ribbon around the rim. Sew the bells to the center of a velveteen ribbon bow with floss. Glue the bow to the front of the topper.

Cutting Board

(also shown on page 81)
- textured cardstock
- tracing paper
- fine-point permanent pen
- scallop-edged scissors
- scrapbook paper
- craft glue
- ¼" dia. jingle bell
- ⅛"w ribbon
- ¼" dia. hole punch
- leather lacing
- paddle cutting board with hole for hanging (ours is 4⅜"x9⅜")
- Grandma's Date-Nut Bread wrapped in plastic wrap (page 81)
- removable tape

1. For the tag, matching short edges, fold a 2½"x4½" cardstock piece in half. Aligning the dashed line with the fold, use the pattern on page 156 and cut a cardstock tag. Write a message inside the tag. Use the scalloped scissors to cut a design from scrapbook paper to fit on the tag; glue to the tag front. Thread the bell onto the center of a 5" ribbon length, tie a bow and glue to the tag front. Punch a hole in the top of the tag.
2. For the hanger, thread an 11" lacing length through the hole in the board, add the tag and knot the lacing ends together.
3. Glue a 2½"x12" scrapbook paper strip to the center of a 3"x12" cardstock strip. Place the bread on the board. Taping the ends at the bottom, wrap the layered strip around the bread and board.

General Instructions

Making Patterns

When the entire pattern is shown, place tracing paper over the pattern and draw over the lines. For a more durable pattern, use a permanent marker to draw over the pattern on stencil plastic.

When only half of the pattern is shown (indicated by a solid blue line on the pattern), fold the tracing paper in half. Place the fold along the solid blue line and trace the pattern half. Turn the folded paper over and draw over the traced lines on the remaining side. Unfold the pattern and cut it out.

Making a Fabric Circle

Matching right sides, fold the fabric square in half from top to bottom and again from left to right. Tie one end of a length of string to a fabric marking pen; insert a thumbtack through the string at the length indicated in the project instructions. Insert the thumbtack through the folded corner of the fabric. Holding the tack in place and keeping the string taut, mark the cutting line (Fig. 1).

Yo-Yos

To make each yo-yo, cut a circle as indicated in the project instructions. Press the circle edge ⅛" to the wrong side and sew *Running Stitches* (page 142) around the edge with a doubled strand of thread. Pull the thread tightly to gather. Knot and trim the thread. Move the small opening to the center of the circle.

Needle Felting

Visit leisurearts.com to view a short needle felting Webcast.

Attach wool felt appliqués, yarn or roving to background fabric using a felting needle tool and mat (Fig 2a). Lightly punch the needles through the wool fibers and background fabric to interlock the fibers and join the pieces without sewing or gluing (Fig 2b). The brush-like mat allows the needles to easily pierce the fibers. We used the Clover Felting Needle Tool to make our projects—it has a locking plastic shield that provides protection from the sharp needles. Felt, wool and woven cotton fabrics all work well as background fabrics.

Felting

Choose an item with wool content of 60% or higher to keep from having to finish the edges.

1. Set your top-loading washing machine for a HOT wash cycle and COLD rinse cycle. Add about a tablespoon of laundry detergent.
2. Place the item in a tight-mesh lingerie or sweater bag (a pillowcase tied at the top works, too!) and toss into the machine. Check every 2-3 minutes during the wash cycle to keep an eye on the amount of felting and the final size. A properly felted item has shrunk to the desired size and the stitches are no longer easy to see. You may want to wear rubber gloves for this, as the water can be very hot.
3. Once the item has felted to your satisfaction, spin out the wash water and then run the item through the cold rinse part of the cycle. To avoid setting permanent creases, don't let the item go through the spin portion of the cycle.
4. While wet, shape the item, stretching it to the finished size. Let the item air dry, which may take a day or two depending on the weather.

Fig. 1

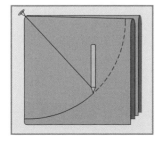

Fig. 2a

Fig. 2b

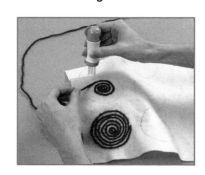

Embroidery Stitches

Blanket Stitch

Referring to Fig. 1, bring the needle up at 1. Keeping the thread below the point of the needle, go down at 2 and come up at 3. Continue working as shown in Fig. 2.

Fig. 1   **Fig. 2**

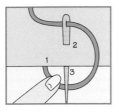

Cross Stitch

Bring the needle up at 1 and go down at 2. Come up at 3 and go down at 4 (Fig. 3).

Fig. 3

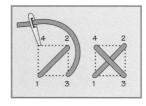

French Knot

Referring to Fig. 4, bring the needle up at 1. Wrap the floss once around the needle and insert the needle at 2, holding the floss end with non-stitching fingers. Tighten the knot; then, pull the needle through the fabric, holding the floss until it must be released. For a larger knot, use more strands; wrap only once.

Fig. 4

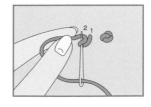

Running Stitch

Referring to Fig. 5, make a series of straight stitches with the stitch length equal to the space between stitches.

Fig. 5

Satin Stitch

Referring to Fig. 6, come up at odd numbers and go down at even numbers with the stitches touching but not overlapping.

Fig. 6

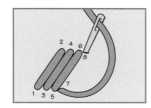

Stem Stitch

Referring to Fig. 7, come up at 1. Keeping the thread below the stitching line, go down at 2 and come up at 3. Go down at 4 and come up at 5.

Fig. 7

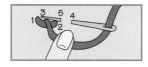

Straight Stitch

Referring to Fig. 8, come up at 1 and go down at 2.

Fig. 8

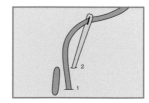

Knit

Abbreviations

cm	centimeters
K	knit
M1	make one
mm	millimeters
P	purl
P2SSO	pass 2 slipped stitches over
Rnd(s)	Round(s)
sp(s)	space(s)
SSK	slip, slip, knit
st(s)	stitch(es)
tog	together

★ — work instructions following ★ as many **more** times as indicated in addition to the first time.

( ) — work enclosed instructions **as many** times as specified by the number immediately following **or** contains explanatory remarks.

colon (:) — the number(s) given after a colon at the end of a row or round denote(s) the number of stitches you should have on that row or round.

work even — work without increasing or decreasing in the established pattern.

Gauge

Exact gauge is essential for proper size. Before beginning your project, make the sample swatch given in the individual instructions in the yarn and needle specified. After completing the swatch, measure it, counting your stitches and rows carefully. If your swatch is larger or smaller than specified, make another, changing needle size to get the correct gauge. Keep trying until you find the size needles that will give you the specified gauge.

Markers

As a convenience to you, we have used markers to help distinguish the beginning of a pattern or round. Place markers as instructed. You may use purchased markers or tie a length of contrasting color yarn around the needle. When you reach a marker on each round, slip it from the left needle to the right needle; remove it when no longer needed.

Knit Increase

Knit the next stitch but do not slip the old stitch off the left needle (Fig. 1a). Insert the right needle into the back loop of the same stitch and knit it (Fig. 1b); then, slip the old stitch off the left needle.

Fig. 1a   **Fig. 1b**

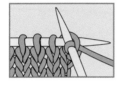

Adding New Stitches

Insert the right needle into stitch as if to **knit**, yarn over and pull the loop through (Fig. 2a); insert the left needle into the loop just worked from **front** to **back** and slip the loop onto the left needle (Fig. 2b). Repeat for the required number of stitches.

Fig. 2a   **Fig. 2b**

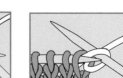

Knit 2 Together
(abbreviated K2 tog)

Insert the right needle into the front of the first two stitches on the left needle as if to **knit** (Fig. 3); then, knit them together as if they were one stitch.

Fig. 3

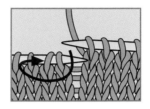

Slip, Slip, Knit (abbreviated SSK)

Separately slip two stitches as if to **knit** (Fig. 4a). Insert the left needle into the front of both slipped stitches (Fig. 4b) and then knit them together as if they were one stitch (Fig. 4c).

Fig. 4a   **Fig. 4b**

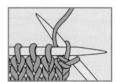 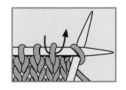

Fig. 4c

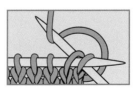

Slip 2, Knit 1, Pass 2 Slipped Stitches Over
(abbreviated slip 2, K1, P2SSO)

With yarn in back, slip two stitches together as if to **knit** (Fig. 5a); then, knit the next stitch. With the left needle, bring both slipped stitches over the knit stitch (Fig. 5b) and off the needle.

Fig. 5a   **Fig. 5b**

 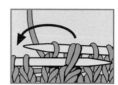

Purl 2 Together
(abbreviated P2 tog)

Insert the right needle into the **front** of the first two stitches on the left needle as if to **purl** (Fig. 6); then, purl them together as if they were one stitch.

Fig. 6

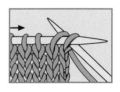

(continued on page 144)

Picking Up Stitches

When instructed to pick up stitches, insert the needle from the front to the back under two strands at the edge of the worked piece (Fig. 7). Put the yarn around the needle as if to knit; then, bring the needle with the yarn back through the stitch to the right side, resulting in a stitch on the needle. Repeat this along the edge, picking up the required number of stitches. A crochet hook may be helpful to pull the yarn through.

Fig. 7

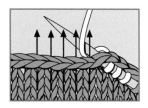

Circular Knitting
Using a Circular Needle

When knitting a tube, as for a hat or mitten, you will work around on the outside of the circle, with the right side of the knitting facing you.

Using a circular needle, cast on all stitches as instructed. Untwist and straighten the stitches on the needle to be sure that the cast on ridge lays on the inside of the needle and never rolls around the needle.

Hold the needle so that the ball of yarn is attached to the stitch closest to the right hand point. Place a marker on the right hand point to mark the beginning of the round.

To begin working in the round, knit the stitches on the left hand point (Fig. 8).

Fig. 8

Continue working each round as instructed without turning the work; but for the first three rounds or so, check to be sure that the cast on edge has not twisted around the needle. If it has, it is impossible to untwist it. The only way to fix this is to rip it out and return to the cast on row.

Using Double-Pointed Needles

When working too few stitches to use a circular needle, double pointed needles are required. Divide the stitches into thirds and slip one-third of the stitches onto each of 3 double-pointed needles, forming a triangle. With the fourth needle, knit across the stitches on the first needle (Fig. 9). You will now have an empty needle with which to knit the stitches from the next needle. Work the first stitch of each needle firmly to prevent gaps.

Fig. 9

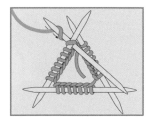

Crochet

Abbreviations

ch(s)	chain(s)
cm	centimeters
dc	double crochet(s)
mm	millimeters
Rnd(s)	Round(s)
sc	single crochet(s)
sp(s)	space(s)
st(s)	stitch(es)
YO	yarn over

★ — work instructions following ★ as many **more** times as indicated in addition to the first time.

( ) — work enclosed instructions **as many** times as specified by the number immediately following **or** work all enclosed instructions in the space indicated **or** contains explanatory remarks.

colon (:) — the number(s) given after a colon at the end of a row or round denote(s) the number of stitches you should have on that row or round.

Gauge

Exact gauge is essential for proper size or fit. Before beginning your project, make the sample swatch given in the individual instructions in the yarn and hook specified. After completing the swatch, measure it, counting your stitches and rows or rounds carefully. If your swatch is larger or smaller than specified, make another, changing hook size to get the correct gauge. Keep trying until you find the size hook that will give you the specified gauge.

Chain

To work a chain stitch, begin with a slip knot on the hook. Bring the yarn **over** the hook from back to front, catching the yarn with the hook and turning the hook slightly toward you to keep the yarn from slipping off. Draw the yarn through the slip knot (Fig. 1) (first chain st made, abbreviated ch).

Fig. 1

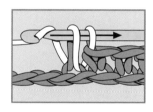

Single Crochet

Insert hook in stitch indicated, YO and pull up a loop, YO and draw through both loops on hook (Fig. 2) (single crochet made, abbreviated sc).

Fig. 2

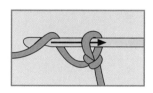

Double Crochet

YO, insert hook in stitch indicated, YO and pull up a loop (3 loops on hook), YO and draw through 2 loops on hook (Fig. 3a), YO and draw through remaining 2 loops on hook (Fig. 3b) (double crochet made, abbreviated dc).

Fig. 3a   Fig. 3b

Back Loop Only

Work only in loop indicated by arrow (Fig. 4).

Fig. 4

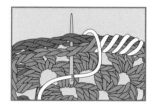

Working in Space Before a Stitch

When instructed to work in a space before a stitch, insert hook in space indicated by arrow (Fig. 5).

Fig. 5

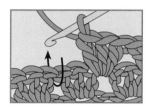

Free Loops of a Chain

When instructed to work in free loops of a chain, work in loop indicated by arrow (Fig. 6).

Fig. 6

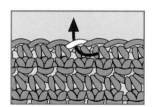

Whipstitch

With **wrong** sides together, sew through both pieces once to secure the beginning of the seam, leaving an ample yarn end to weave in later. Insert the needle from **right** to **left** through one strand on each piece (Fig. 7). Bring the needle around and insert it from **right** to **left** through the next strand on both pieces. Repeat along the edge, being careful to match stitches and rows.

Fig. 7

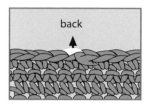

Joining with Sc

When instructed to join with sc, begin with a slip knot on the hook. Insert the hook in the stitch or space indicated, YO and pull up a loop, YO and draw through both loops on the hook.

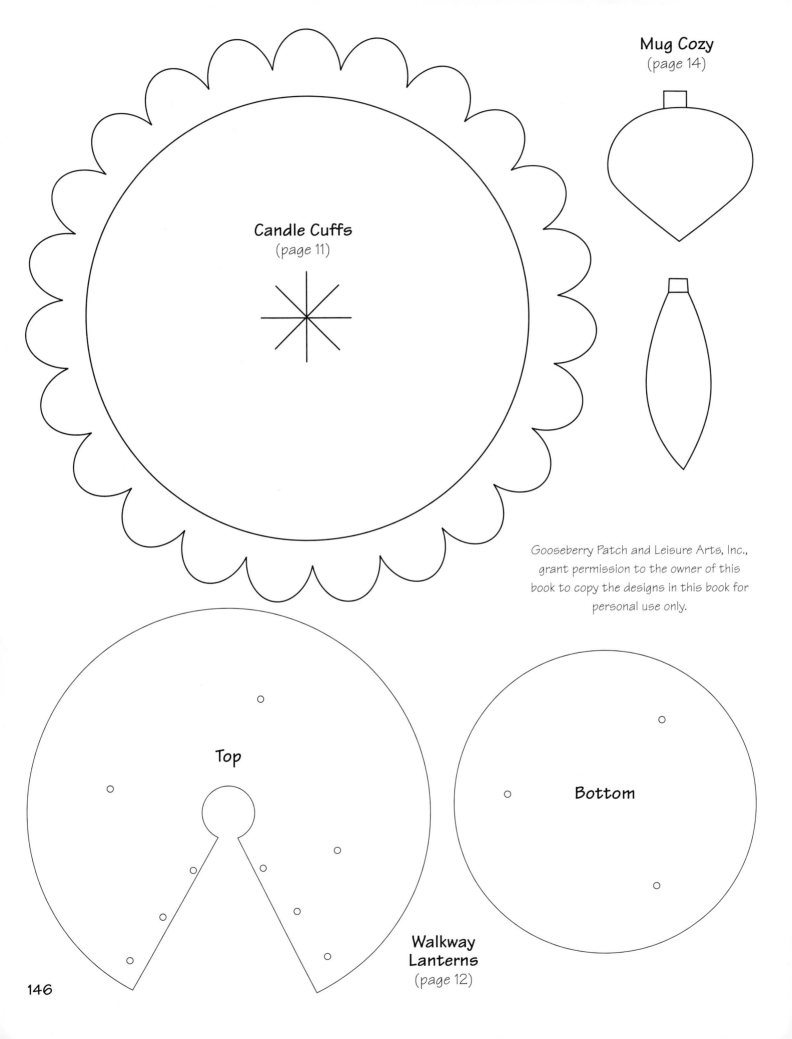

Candle Cuffs
(page 11)

Mug Cozy
(page 14)

Gooseberry Patch and Leisure Arts, Inc., grant permission to the owner of this book to copy the designs in this book for personal use only.

Top

Bottom

Walkway Lanterns
(page 12)

Tree Skirt
(page 19)

You know Vixen

Wave

Dasher

Prancer

Comet

Cupid

Donner

Vixen

148

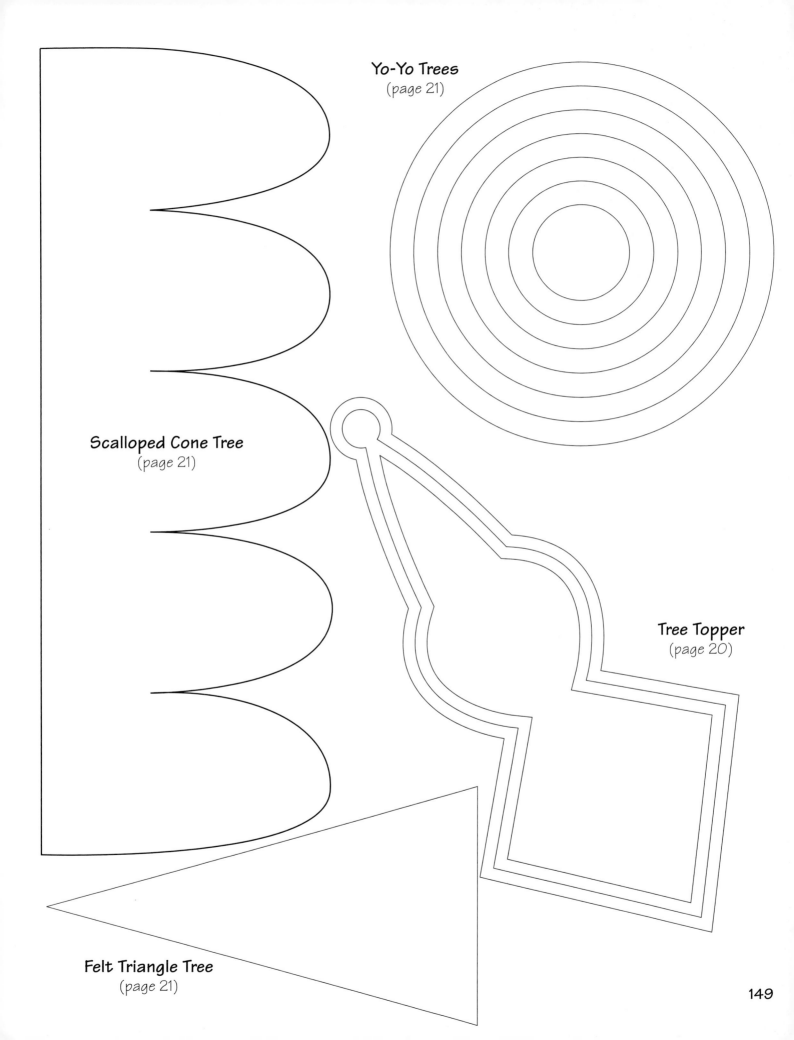

Yo-Yo Trees
(page 21)

Scalloped Cone Tree
(page 21)

Tree Topper
(page 20)

Felt Triangle Tree
(page 21)

Holly Pillow
(page 35)

Corduroy Stocking &
Zigzag Stocking
(page 37)

Welcome Sign
(page 30)

Welcome

Embroidered Framed Piece
(page 32)

At Christmas play and make good cheer, for Christmas comes but once a year.

—Thomas Tusser

Santa Doll
(page 40)

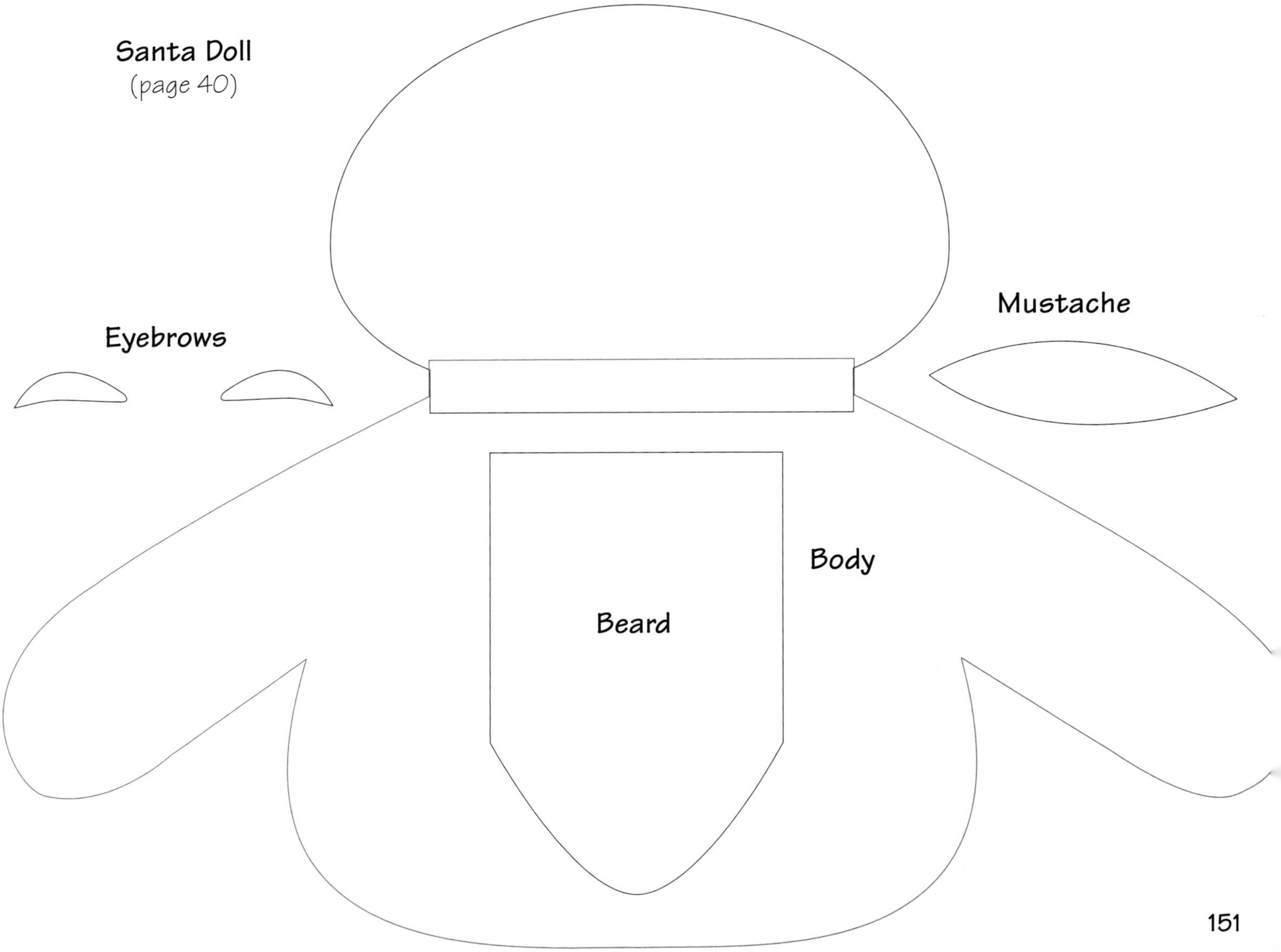

Eyebrows

Mustache

Body

Beard

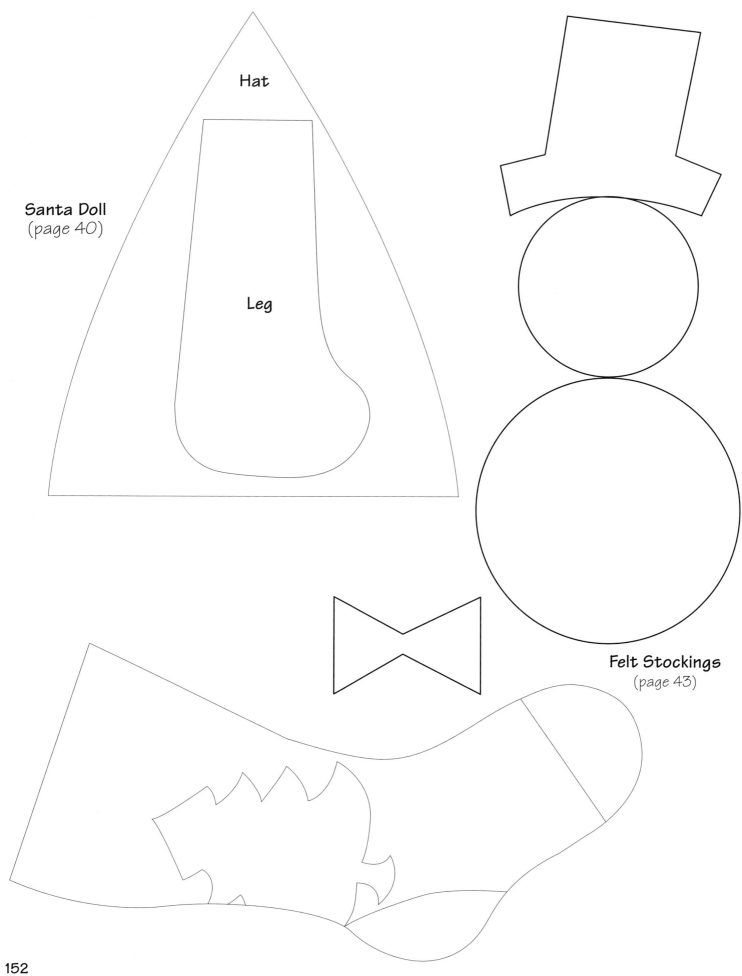

Santa Doll
(page 40)

Hat

Leg

Felt Stockings
(page 43)

152

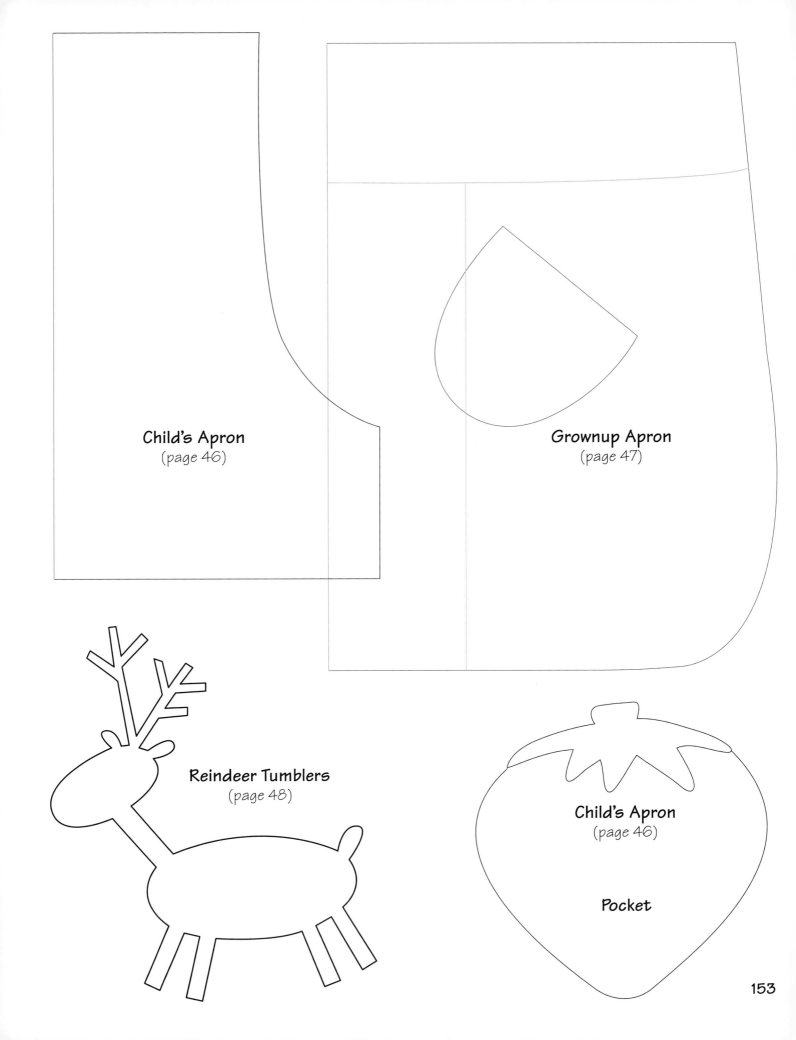

Child's Apron
(page 46)

Grownup Apron
(page 47)

Reindeer Tumblers
(page 48)

Child's Apron
(page 46)

Pocket

Tea Gift Set
(page 77)

Flip-Flop Doll
(page 56)

Appliquéd Jacket
(page 53)

Flip-Flop Doll
(page 56)

Pincushions
(page 57)

Yellow

Blue

Muff
(page 54)

Pink

155

Gardener's
Gift Set
(page 58)

No matter how long the winter, spring is sure to follow.

Photo Window Card
(page 64)

Package Wraps
(page 70)

Cutting Board
(page 81)

Lunch Box
(page 79)

Fabric-Covered
Canister
(page 67)

Peppermint Package
(page 74)

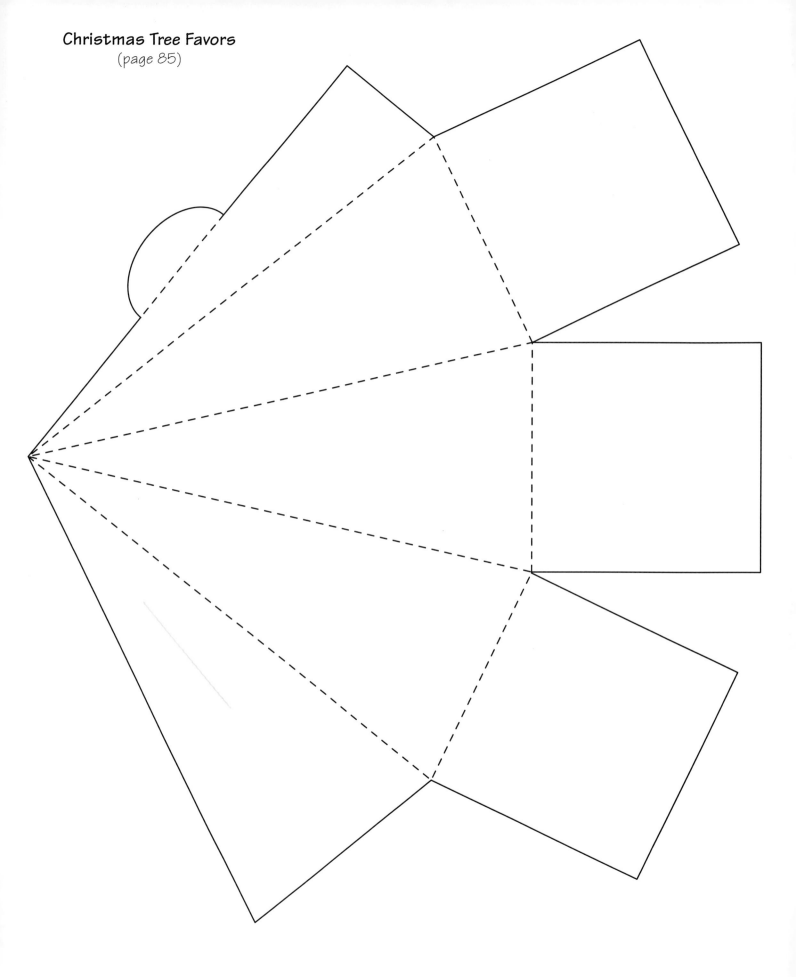

Project Index

Recipe Index

Credits

We want to extend a warm thank you to the people who allowed us to photograph some of our projects at their homes: Alda Ellis, Christy Myers, Nancy Porter and Elizabeth Rice.

We want to especially thank Mark Mathews Photography and Ken West Photography for their excellent work.

We would like to recognize the following companies for providing some of the materials and tools we used to make our projects: Lion Brand® Yarn Company and Patons Yarn for yarn; Saral® Paper Corporation for transfer paper; The DMC Corporation for embroidery floss; and Clover Needlecraft, Inc. for the felting needle tool, mat and wool roving.

Special thanks go to Marianna Crowder for crocheting the Felted Granny Square Tote and Ripple Crocheted Throw and to Raymelle Greening and Sue Galucki for knitting the Winter Warmers.

If these cozy Christmas ideas have inspired you to look for more Gooseberry Patch® publications, treat yourself to a Gooseberry Patch product catalog, which is filled with cookbooks, candles, enamelware, bowls, gourmet goodies and hundreds of other country collectibles. For a subscription to "A Country Store in Your Mailbox©," visit www.gooseberrypatch.com.